INSIGHTS INTO THE RUGBY WORLD CUP

INSIGHTS
into the
RUGBY
World Cup

NICK MALLETT
with LLOYD BURNARD

JONATHAN BALL PUBLISHERS
JOHANNESBURG • CAPE TOWN

Published in South Africa in 2023 by
JONATHAN BALL PUBLISHERS
A division of Media24 (Pty) Ltd
PO Box 33977
Jeppestown
2043

ISBN 978-1-77619-297-7
ebook ISBN 978-1-77619-298-4

*Every effort has been made to trace the copyright holders and
to obtain their permission for the use of copyright material.
The publishers apologise for any errors or omissions and would
be grateful to be notified of any corrections that should be
incorporated in future editions of this book.*

www.jonathanball.co.za
www.twitter.com/JonathanBallPub
www.facebook.com/JonathanBallPublishers

Cover by mrdesign
Design and typesetting by Martine Barker
Cover image by Nardus Engelbrecht
Printed and bound by CTP Printers, Cape Town
Set in Adobe Jenson Pro

Contents

Preface:
A sporting spectacle is born

I can still remember the smell of the crisp Cape Town air as I walked through the Newlands gates with 43 000 other fans, mostly South African, about to witness a game that would change rugby forever. It was 18 June 1995, and this was the Rugby World Cup semifinal between England and New Zealand. Nobody could have predicted what was to come.

I had been coaching at False Bay Rugby Club in Constantia, Cape Town, which still holds such a dear place in my heart, and I was finalising the paperwork with Boland to start my first major head coaching job on South African soil. I had been asked by the SABC – I think by legendary anchor Trevor Quirk – to cover the semifinal for live radio. It was a huge honour as I had never done any broadcasting or commentary before, apart from maybe one Western Province game for television.

I had one of the best seats in the house, right on the halfway line, and it was such a magical experience for me. I never imagined then that in just four years' time, I would be taking the Springboks to the 1999 World Cup as defending champions. I was at Newlands as a rugby fan that day, taking in every cheer and tackle, living the moment with everybody else.

When most of us fondly remember the 1995 Rugby World Cup, we think immediately of Joel Stransky's famous drop goal in the final – one of the most iconic moments in South Africa's sporting history – and a Springbok triumph that shook the nation. It was a fantastic World Cup for a range of reasons, and from a South African point of view it unified our national team and our country; largely down to President Nelson Mandela's support for the side, who won it as underdogs.

'Nelson, Nelson, Nelson!' the crowd chanted at Newlands when the president walked onto the field before a tournament opener in which the Springboks stunned the defending champions, Australia. It was spine-tingling stuff, and still one of the most emotional moments I can recall. I had been out of the country for about 10 years, coaching in France, and to come back and see such warmth for the leader of our nation was nothing short of sensational.

I was in the Railway Stand as a spectator for that game, and when Pieter Hendriks rounded David Campese down the left flank to score, pumping his fist in the air, there was an overwhelming sense of national unity welling up that would become part of the fabric of a tournament that gave birth to the new era of Springbok rugby.

Mandela's courage in supporting the Springbok team, given the history of rugby and the way it had evolved into an Afrikaner sport, was astounding. There was suddenly huge support for the Springboks, and that certainly wasn't the case when I left South Africa in 1985. Back then, the majority of South Africans – who were not white – supported overseas teams, and understandably so. But in 1995, because of a democratic government and a president who backed the team, the crowd was fully behind the Springboks.

By the time the All Blacks met England in the semifinal, the Springboks had already beaten France in the Durban mud the night before to book their spot at Ellis Park against the winners. Most would have expected New Zealand to beat England, which they did, but the performance of one man stood out, breathing life into rugby and the sport's showpiece event.

His name was Jonah Lomu, and he was just 20 years old.

Rugby had reached the point where it needed more. There were skilled players who had succeeded at the 1987 and 1991 World Cups – Campese, the joint leading try scorer in his side's victorious 1991 campaign, immediately comes to mind – but there was something missing. In terms of playing styles and hype, the 1987 and 1991 tournaments hadn't offered much that was different from what we were seeing in June/July tours and regular Test fixtures.

That all changed on this glorious day at Newlands.

England went into the match confident they were going to beat New Zealand, but four superb Lomu tries later – two in each half – they had fallen to a 45-29 defeat, beaten by one man. It was one of those 'I was there' moments. It was so ahead of its time, and it had such an influence in showing people what rugby could become.

From that moment, the game became about packed stadiums and the chance to see phenomenal athletes perform. There was so much in the 1995 World Cup that was good from a South African point of view, but what triggered the momentum for professional rugby, in my opinion, was the spectacle of seeing Jonah Lomu with a rugby ball under his arm, scattering defenders. He was a force of nature the likes of which I had never seen before.

Former Wallabies prop Ewen McKenzie once told a story that has always stayed with me. Australia were playing the All Blacks in a Bledisloe Cup match and

Lomu took a short pass from about 10 metres out. McKenzie was defending and felt it would be a routine tackle. He set himself, got nice and low, and all he saw coming at him was the point of Lomu's shoulder and his knee, almost touching each other. McKenzie could not see a waist, and everything about Lomu's positioning was loaded with intent. The prop was knocked flat on his backside and Lomu scored. When you have 120 kg coming at you in under 11 seconds for the 100 metres, it is very difficult to stop.

Whenever he got the ball, Lomu simply shrugged players off. Ray Mordt, who played 18 times for the Springboks between 1980 and 1984, was a player with a reputation for bouncing players off him as an exceptional carrier. But Ray was probably 90-odd kilograms; Lomu was around 30 kg heavier, and just as fast.

Lomu was originally identified as a No. 8 but he didn't have the endurance of a loose forward, who has to keep going for 80 minutes. On the wing, he was able to execute powerful surges and recover in between them. With that sort of pace, he was almost impossible to stop.

I had seen him on television before the semifinal against England, and I thought it was just bad defence that had allowed him to score so freely. But when you saw him live, as I did that day, you realised it had absolutely nothing to do with defensive shortcomings. The English were trying their best to get a hand on him, but he had such powerful thighs and explosive speed that if you didn't get both legs at knee level, he was going to bounce you off.

He had long arms, huge legs and driving hips, and he could swerve and beat you with pace when he needed. That is what made him so difficult, and Jeremy Guscott and the other English players were brave in trying to defend him. Mike Catt put himself directly in front of Lomu, not giving an inch, and it was like he had been hit by a bus that ran right over him. It was the most incredible try.

By the time the final came around, Lomu had been scoring tries against everybody he had played with ease. It seemed so straightforward. The All Blacks were playing quality rugby as it was, but they started using Lomu at every possible opportunity because he was simply a phenomenon.

It was the courage of the team that stood out for the Springboks in the final. Joost van der Westhuizen and Japie Mulder put in tackles on Lomu that would be replayed countless times in the years to come, and even a few of the forwards got involved in defending against Lomu. The whole team were focused on not allowing this one guy to score.

The ability of one individual to dominate the sport the way Lomu did in 1995 turned rugby into a global game. Hell, after the World Cup there was even a Jonah

Lomu video game. He became a global star. Even though South Africa won the World Cup in the end, Lomu was all the rugby community could talk about.

By the time it came to 1999, Lomu could still score the most unbelievable tries, but people had worked him out a bit and identified weaknesses in his defensive game that could be exploited. His contribution to the sport was immeasurable.

Lomu was a critical pivot in changing rugby from ticking along as an amateur sport in which most of the money went to the unions but not the players. After Lomu, rugby players became superstars who found themselves on the front pages of newspapers, and things have never been the same.

Immediately after 1995, professionalism kicked in. Media tycoon Rupert Murdoch tried to buy rugby, in the way Kerry Packer had done with cricket, and SA Rugby Union president Louis Luyt got the Springboks together under captain Francois Pienaar and encouraged them to stay within the fold. They agreed, and from that moment on rugby players were paid for being entertainers.

Fans understood that you came to watch games because of the players, not because of the beautiful stadiums or the administrators. Rugby would have looked very different had the Murdoch deal gone through, and while the Springboks played a key part in how things unfolded, the game was given that injection of independence by what Lomu did at the World Cup.

His contribution should never be forgotten. And as we look ahead to the 10th Rugby World Cup and unpack everything that makes France 2023 the most exciting tournament yet, we should do so in the knowledge that one man – no longer with us – shaped where we are and this game that we all love so much.

1
The magic of the World Cup

There is no country that typifies the magic of the Rugby World Cup more than South Africa. I may be biased in that assessment, but having experienced the triumphs of 1995, 2007 and 2019, I am confident in making it. The unique history of this country, and what those wins did for us as a nation, make it so.

The 2007 victory by Jake White's Springboks did not have anywhere near the same social impact as the championship sides of 1995 and 2019, but there will always be an overwhelming sense of pride that comes with being the best on the planet, and South Africans love winning more than most! When the Springboks are on top of the world, that filters down into society.

However, with every ecstatic winner comes a devastated loser, and I know that aspect of the World Cup better than most. Taking the Springboks to the World

Cup in 1999 will forever remain my greatest honour in the game, and coming so close to achieving something special and falling agonisingly short – as we did in the Twickenham semifinal against Australia that was decided in extra time – is something words can never fully describe. I still think about it and, while 1999 was not meant to be for us, so many wonderful memories were created over that period and they will stay with me for the rest of my life.

I watched the first two Rugby World Cups on television: 1987 in New Zealand and Australia (won by New Zealand), and 1991 in England, Scotland, Wales, Ireland and France (won by Australia). They were impressive tournaments, and as I followed their progress there was always the feeling that the southern hemisphere teams – New Zealand and Australia – were stronger than the rest.

They were 'World Cups', but in those days they were certainly not as wide open as the tournament is now. They were still exciting, but I didn't get the feeling of an inclusive international competition where nations from all corners of the globe competed for rugby's ultimate prize. That only came in 1995.

One guy who doesn't get a lot of credit when people talk about South Africa's post-apartheid rugby history is Edward Griffiths, the SA Rugby CEO in 1995. Movies have been made and books have been written about the Springbok win that year, but they don't tell the story of how important Griffiths was in nurturing the mature way in which the Springboks engaged with the South African population during that time.

'One team, one country' was his brainchild, and he encouraged captain Francois Pienaar and team manager Morné du Plessis to seek the assistance of President Nelson Mandela to ensure the government's support. Griffiths understood the importance of making the Boks the champions of the people: all South Africans, not just the white rugby-watching part of the population.

The World Cup in 1995, and the birth of *World in Union* (the song that became the tournament's anthem), saw an influx of hundreds of thousands of international tourists to South African shores. This was a global event, and for the first time the World Cup had the international appeal of its billing.

Given the South African situation and how sensitive everything was – some white South Africans were still waving old flags and refusing to sing any anthem other than *Die Stem* – it was incredibly brave of Mandela to back the Boks in the way he did.

When I was coach of the Springboks in 1998, and after we'd had 17 Test wins in a row, I was fortunate enough to meet Madiba. Springbok captain Gary Teichmann, the management and I were invited to lunch with the great man, and we were given an hour with him.

We were all nervous and excited at the prospect of meeting the father of our nation, but we had no need to be. Madiba was so humble, kind and caring, and he made us all feel at ease and welcome. He enjoyed the conversation so much that we ended up being there for two hours.

I asked him about the period before the 1995 World Cup and what the feeling had been in the country back then, and he told me a story that placed the enormity of what he had done for South African rugby into perspective.

Some months before the tournament, Mandela had to go to KwaZulu-Natal to give an address at an ANC function, and he told his audience he was backing the Springboks. He was very honest and told me how he was booed when he went onto that Durban stage wearing a Springbok cap. He waited for a moment of silence, and he went on to say that we were one country and that no matter what the Bok emblem represented before 1992, there was now a need to support all national teams. He declared his support for the Springboks there, in that room, long before the 1995 World Cup.

He said it was a very difficult moment for him. It was such a tense time, and it could so easily have gone the wrong way. I felt that the sensitivity with which the emergence of the new Springbok setup was handled by Edward Griffiths, Morné du Plessis, coach Kitch Christie and Francois Pienaar had gone a long way, but ultimately the success of the project was down to having a president who was so forgiving. Mandela saw the bigger, long-term picture of rugby being a force for good in the country, not something we should bash on the head because of what had happened in the past.

When you combine all that – which was essentially South Africa growing up and maturing into an understanding of its own democracy – and you put it together with the international support that flooded into the country, the 1995 World Cup was always going to be special. During that period between 25 May and 24 June, it felt as if South Africa was living in an incredibly rarefied time when everything was going well for us.

We had the most respected president in the world running our country, we were back playing international sport and we had an opportunity to host a World Cup we had never even participated in. South Africa was buzzing! There was a warmth from the foreign visitors, saying what a beautiful country we had, and that wasn't something we were used to. On the field we were by no means the favourites, but Bok supporters were so passionate and caught up in the moment that they always believed we were in with an outside chance.

By the time the Springboks reached the final against the All Blacks, the 1995 showpiece had already succeeded as a celebration of South Africa. When I arrived at

Ellis Park a few hours before kickoff, again working as a radio commentator for the SABC, the atmosphere was electric.

Who could forget the South African Airways Boeing 747 that flew over the stadium? Then there was the roar when Mandela walked onto the field. It was jaw-dropping to realise how popular he was and how everyone – black and white – embraced him. There was such a massive leap forward for South Africa that day, and it probably all happened a bit too fast when you look back at it. It was almost a fairy tale.

The game went into extra time and, of course, Joel Stransky kicked *that* drop goal and we hung on to win. It was beyond anyone's expectations and the most incredibly unifying experience South African sport had ever seen. The Boks' victory felt like a miracle. They were not the best team at the tournament but they were the best on the day, and there was this inexplicable determination not to lose and to deny New Zealand even one try.

When you talk to the All Blacks who played in that game, as I have done, they admit they were confident going in. But on the field they felt this momentum building in the whole country, driving the Boks on, and they simply couldn't break down the players in green and gold. There was so much belief. To see the celebrations in the streets that night was amazing. People were dancing and hugging strangers, and it was a truly magical, historic moment.

Reality inevitably hits, however, and the euphoria did not last forever. Everyone went back to their normal lives, so it would be naive to say this win transformed South Africa. But it showed what the country could be, even if only for that brief period of 24 or 48 hours.

Everybody was so proud to be part of this new journey that, at the time, promised so much for the nation. I felt that so powerfully, especially when Francois Pienaar famously said after the final: 'We didn't have 60 000 South Africans [at Ellis Park], we had 43 million South Africans.'

That quote captured how the team felt about playing for their country, and it set the standard for what playing in a World Cup means today. I remember being in tears watching it all unfold, seeing the disbelief on the faces of the South Africans on the field and in the crowd, savouring this extraordinary moment.

It was an unbelievable experience.

From then on, the World Cup became the goal for every rugby player on the planet. It was South Africa's time to celebrate, but 1995 left every other team – the All Blacks, Australians, French, English and Irish – wanting that success and that same golden moment. It was the catalyst that slowly but surely led to an improvement in standards across the board. Now, in 2023, we have a World Cup that is as open as it has ever been.

All rugby players have goals when they turn professional, but after 1995 there was no doubt in my mind that they were now all focused primarily on where they would be in four years' time, and how they could make sure they were at their physical peak and available for selection to represent their country at a World Cup. That immediately became the pinnacle of the sport.

At every World Cup since, players from all over the world – Jonny Wilkinson, Dan Carter, Stephen Larkham, Cheslin Kolbe – have had their legacies defined and solidified by incredible performances in a tournament that has become the pinnacle of international rugby.

Nothing matters more and, while what happens on the field ultimately determines that greatness, it is how much it all means to those watching that gives it that weight of importance.

Before Rassie Erasmus was named coach of the Springboks in 2018, he invited me, Carel du Plessis and Andre Markgraaff to supper in Stellenbosch with him and his assistants, Jacques Nienaber and Mzwandile Stick. He wanted to ask the ex-coaches he had played under where he would encounter the biggest stumbling blocks when he took over the job.

I raised the issue of transformation, telling Rassie this would be one of the most important elements of his tenure. If the Springboks won but were not transformed, it would not be enough; Rassie would face a torrent of criticism.

He was way ahead of me. Without even flinching, Rassie looked me dead in the eye and told me what he was going to do. 'We will transform, and we will win,' he said, confidently. 'I know the players I am going to select, and I want them because I believe they are the best in their position.'

It was such a clear answer. He wasn't hedging his bets at all. He knew exactly where he was going, and he was fully aware of the importance of winning the World Cup with a side that represented the whole of South Africa – not just the powerful minority. If he was going to do this, he was going to bring the whole country along for the ride, and that is exactly what he did.

The 1995 World Cup was an eye-opener for South Africa, and the outpouring of joy after the victory meant there was not much concern that the team were untransformed. But by 2019, there had been regular criticism that Springbok teams at the World Cup were too white. This drew negative reactions from politicians and those who wanted rugby to be for everyone, and rightly so.

The 2019 team were remarkable in the sense that even before they left for the World Cup in Japan, they were fully accepted and supported by our most contentious politicians. One of the reasons for that lay in a decision Rassie told me about during that dinner in Stellenbosch: he was going to make Siya Kolisi his captain. While it was a massive step in the right direction in terms of winning over strong black support and making this a team that represented the real South Africa, not just a select few, this decision by Rassie was based only on Kolisi's merit as a world-class flanker and leader. I have no doubt about that.

There were players in that squad from all corners of the country – farms, suburbs and townships – and Rassie was adamant from the beginning that such inclusion was imperative. By having those players in the squad and by winning in 2019, there was a genuine groundswell of support for the Springboks from the majority of South Africans. Perhaps for the first time, President Mandela's request 24 years earlier – for the entire nation to support the Springboks – had finally been answered.

While 1995 was groundbreaking for many reasons, there still wasn't the feeling afterwards that rugby was a game for everyone. But that all changed when Kolisi lifted the Webb Ellis Cup on 2 November 2019 in Yokohama. There was a level of emotion attached to the win that would have left even South Africa's strongest contingent of All Black supporters finding it really difficult not to celebrate.

One try in the final was created by Lukhanyo Am and scored by Makazole Mapimpi, and the other by

Cheslin Kolbe – all players of colour. It was the most powerful statement our South African team could have made.

Going into the 2019 World Cup, there was no talk of the Springboks being contenders; especially after they lost their opening game against New Zealand. I was at the quarterfinal against Japan in Chōfu and it felt like every non-South African supporter in the world wanted the Boks to lose. To get through that in the calm manner they did, with the match being close at halftime, was superb from Rassie and the team. It was the same in the semifinal against Wales, a match that was such a stern examination of composure.

In the week before the final, the talk was that there was only one team in it. I was in the country as part of World Rugby's refereeing selection committee, and the feeling from so many was that it was simply a question of by how many points England were going to win.

The Boks had scraped through their semifinal while England had delivered one of the great World Cup knockout displays to beat New Zealand 19-7, so there was a very one-sided view on the final from objective observers.

I did a television segment with Hanyani Shimange in which we talked to former England centre Will Greenwood, and Greenwood rattled off all the reasons

England were going to take the Boks apart. Shimmy and I agreed that England would go in as favourites, given how they had played in the semifinal, but we pointed out to Greenwood that they hadn't faced a Springbok pack in a scrumming contest, or a Springbok defence that could get off the line quickly and give no time on the ball. South Africa, we told him, were certainly in with a chance, and it was a very quiet press box when the Boks won 32-12.

However, the real victory in 2019 took place not in Japan but at home. When the Boks returned, they were embraced by every single sports-loving South African. They had shown what South Africans can do when there is guidance, direction, respect, support and the right people in the right positions at the right time. Why couldn't the Boks, and the way the team pulled together against all the odds, be an example of what South Africa could be like as a society?

I know that isn't what Rassie was trying to do with this team, but for those of us who saw what they achieved and how they played, it was easy to make the comparison. This triumph, as much as it was rightly celebrated, was a stark reminder of what we could be – and what we weren't – outside of our rugby team.

In a country so often filled with doom and gloom, the Boks of 2019 were the brightest of lights, breaking down barriers and pulling an entire nation together. That is the power of the Rugby World Cup.

The Springboks of 2007 often get lost in this discussion as we rightly celebrate the defining achievements of 1995 and 2019, and that isn't necessarily fair. Winning a World Cup is an incredible feat that most players and coaches will never experience, and it is not easy.

Many people forget that the build-up to that 2007 World Cup (also in France) was far from ideal for the Boks, and that Jake White had endured a hugely testing 2006. In a July Tri-Nations match, the Boks had been hammered 49-0 by the Wallabies in Brisbane. Then, on their end-of-year tour, White was made to return home before his players to face a vote of no confidence after losses to Ireland and England.

Jake has always been a dedicated and successful coach, and after surviving the vote he dusted himself off, stuck to his plan and got the job done. The Springboks were the best team at that tournament by some distance.

White's relationship with his captain, John Smit, was very close. He had so much confidence in Smit's ability and backed him to the hilt when there were loud calls for other hookers to start, and that made the taste of victory especially sweet.

South Africa erupted after that clinical win in the final over England. Some of the players in the 2007 team were among the very best to have worn Springbok colours. All solidified their status as legends of the game.

Going to the 1999 edition when I was coach, every single player understood what this tournament meant to the guys who won it in 1995. Whether they were brilliant rugby players or not, the class of '95 were a winning team who had secured their legendary status in South African rugby, and none of that was lost on the squad that travelled to Europe in 1999. We understood the enormity of what we were trying to do, which was to defend our crown away from home.

We had a tough draw – England in the quarterfinals, Australia in the semifinals – but we had the players to achieve our goal. The beauty of World Cup rugby, though, is that it often comes down to an opportunity taken or an opportunity lost. That can be the only difference between getting through a tough semifinal or being knocked out, and our team knew that, too.

We knew we were not going to run away with any game and that we would have to take the opportunities when they came. We knew that what we were doing had the power to forever change the lives of every member of the squad. There was pressure, but it wasn't bad pressure. It was something you wanted. You wanted to feel nervous and excited, and to understand that you were representing an entire country of passionate supporters back home.

I was incredibly proud. The team had enjoyed such a lot of success in 1997 and 1998, and then obviously we went through some issues. Dropping Gary Teichmann as my captain before the tournament was a mistake I later acknowledged and still regret, and while it proved difficult for the team and me to handle, there was still an overwhelming belief that we could achieve something special and build on the legacy of 1995.

It felt as though the 1999 World Cup only really started for us in the week before we played England in the quarterfinals. We had beaten Scotland in our tournament opener, but the other group-stage fixtures were relatively routine wins and we slipped underneath the radar for much of those middle stages of the competition.

Once we reached the quarterfinals, we knew it was going to get tough. England was rigorously drilled and coached, and was playing so well.

In the week leading up to the tournament, we had an injury to our fly half, Henry Honiball, which was really disappointing because he was probably the first name I would put down on my Springbok team sheet. I had so much respect for him as a rugby player and as a fly half, as well for his ability as a defender, and so did the team. When people turned around and saw Henry with the No. 10 on his back, it made everybody else play 10 per cent better.

After he tore his hamstring at the beginning of the competition, Jannie de Beer filled in for him and did an excellent job, but going into the quarterfinal against England we weren't creating the try-scoring opportunities we could with Henry, who would take it very flat to the line. It was a source of concern for us.

On the Wednesday before the game, we had a rest day when players could relax and do what they liked. About eight of us decided to play golf and I shared a cart with Brendan Venter, playing with Jannie and Joost van der Westhuizen.

I chatted to Brendan about the England game, saying I was worried we weren't creating enough opportunities to score tries. He gave me a very simple answer, telling me Jannie de Beer couldn't be asked to play like Henry Honiball. And it was Brendan who first made me aware of Jannie's incredible ability to kick drop goals.

I called De Beer over and said: 'Jannie, I hear you like kicking drop goals.'

'Ja, I do,' he replied.

'But I haven't seen you kick one drop goal – at training or on the park – the whole tournament,' I told him.

'Ja, because you've been asking me to play like Henry Honiball.' It was a very good retort.

We needed points, so when we got back to the training ground the next day we set up scenarios to test Jannie's drop goals and see if they could work for us. I remember that training session so vividly. He was so confident. We must have given him eight different positions on the field and he kicked over every single drop goal.

By the time we got to the quarterfinal, we were sold on our game plan. Never again have I seen a display of drop kicking like the one Jannie produced that day. There were five De Beer drop goals – a world record – and suddenly, we were in the semifinal.

Then I had a dilemma. Henry Honiball was fit again, but Jannie had just played the game of his life. It was such a complicated problem for me, but what happened next was something that has stayed with me as a moment that perfectly illustrates what it means to represent your country at this great tournament.

When I told Henry I was considering picking him at fly half for the semifinal, his reply was that it would not be fair on Jannie, who he felt should play ahead of him. Henry further argued that the team would not understand it if Jannie was dropped after playing the whole tournament and having just had the game of his life, and he wanted to see his teammate rewarded after what he had achieved in the quarters. After careful tactical consideration, I agreed. How could I argue with that logic?

It was such a humbling moment of selflessness: Henry was essentially giving up an opportunity to play in a World Cup semifinal because of what he felt the team needed most.

That whole week, all we read about and talked about was Saturday's game at Twickenham. Every single player was completely aware of his moment in time. We had already played Australia three times that season, so we knew they were a tough side to beat. We had beaten them and they had beaten us, but none of that mattered. We would have to be at our very best to win, and we were in the game from start to finish.

Our defence was outstanding, bar one or two lapses, but we were up for it. There were no tries, and while penalties were being exchanged neither side could build a commanding or comfortable lead. The Wallabies were kicking everything deep into our half, trying to avoid the possibility of a drop goal from Jannie, and they were 18-15 ahead when we were awarded a penalty in the last minute of the game.

It was on the right-hand side of the field, near the 40-metre line, right in front of where I was sitting. Without any hesitation, Jannie grabbed the ball and called for a shot at poles. The wind was blowing directly into his face and the angle was not in his favour. Nothing about that moment suggested this was going over, except for the fact that the man kicking the ball was Jannie de Beer. The ball did not deviate on its way between the posts, and for him to be as cool as that under pressure was staggering.

As a coach, you believe in all sorts of things. Some fall back on religion, others trust to luck, but I was pretty fatalistic about things as the game headed into extra time. I remember thinking: 'What god would allow us to kick that over and still not win this game?' It seemed like it was meant to be.

It wasn't. Stephen Larkham's extra-time drop goal was a dagger to the heart, in the same way I imagine the Wallabies felt when Jannie kicked his penalty.

We found out after the game that Larkham was actually trying to kick the ball dead so we would have a 22-metre dropout and the Wallabies could gain a bit of territory. It was one of those ridiculous sporting moments. The ball fell sideways but he hit it so flush. I've seen it in slow motion so many times. It started 10 metres outside the right-hand upright, hooked around and somehow went straight between the poles. Unreal.

It is impossible to describe the feeling in the changing room after that game. It was as if there had been a death in the family. There was silence. The players looked at the floor, shellshocked by how close they had come to a World Cup final, only to have it ripped away from them. Os du Randt was in tears, and he wasn't the only one. It was a horrendous moment, and we knew the people back home were so disappointed.

After the semifinal, Jannie came to me and begged me to play Henry Honiball in the third-place playoff against the All Blacks. Like Henry had done earlier, Jannie was putting the team first, believing everyone would get the lift they needed for the All Blacks if Henry returned.

It's one of the greatest things I've witnessed. It was two men, each giving up his place without knowing the other player had done exactly the same, all for the benefit of the team. I often think about the selflessness those two showed.

We picked ourselves up for the third-place game and New Zealand couldn't do the same after their semifinal defeat to France. We won 22-18, and I was proud of that.

The day the Springboks were eliminated from the Rugby World Cup for the first time, 30 October 1999, also happened to be my 43rd birthday. It is one I will never forget. But even with that devastating defeat, I look back on the journey and am filled with nothing but honour, pride and gratitude.

I had the opportunity to experience the magic of the Rugby World Cup – the highs, the lows, the cheers and the tears. I wouldn't change it for the world.

2
The Springbok World Cup machine

The Springboks will enter the 2023 World Cup in France as defending champions, and while they have an incredibly difficult draw they will back themselves to beat anybody.

This is the most open World Cup yet and several sides are in with a shot, but South Africa will know that if they perform to their full potential they will be right in the mix. I certainly feel they can go the distance again. It has almost always been that way; even when they haven't been in the best shape, South African rugby sides have found a way to turn it on at World Cups.

But the 2023 Boks are respected as one of the most feared, dangerous and difficult-to-beat sides in the world, thanks to the work done under Rassie Erasmus and Jacques Nienaber.

In their seven World Cup appearances, the Springboks have never been eliminated in the group stages. They have won the tournament three times, finished third twice and have been losing quarterfinalists twice. That is a very impressive record, and one that contributes immensely to the proud tradition of Springbok rugby. So, what is it that makes the Boks such a force at the Rugby World Cup?

Ultimately – and this should not come as any surprise – it comes down to physicality. While the Springboks were not invited to play in the 1987 or 1991 editions, the rugby development of this nation goes back decades.

In the South African context such trips down memory lane are never comfortable if we acknowledge our awful history of exclusion, and the truth is that rugby in this country was an elitist sport. Black players could not represent the Springboks, and that was a travesty of justice that the whole world, and what was then the International Rugby Board (now World Rugby), would not accept. Eventually, and thankfully, that changed in the early 1990s with the birth of democracy, and while black players were then allowed to play at the highest level, a South African playing culture had long been identified.

Historically, the Afrikaners had found rugby to be a sport they were very good at; more importantly, it was one in which they felt they could beat the English at school and club levels. It took a long time after the

South African War, which ended in 1902, for tensions between the English and the Afrikaners to settle. They were separate cultures in South Africa, and while they had rugby in common it was accepted that the sport was a perfect fit for the Afrikaners' physicality and size. The Dutch have always been the tallest population in Europe, and they have always produced big babies who grow into strong men.

Rugby is a sport that favours big, physical and fast players. You can have small, agile players who prove successful but there is no question that big, strong, quick players who have ball skills will be in an advantageous position, especially in their formative years.

Two cultures that physically fit that mould are the Afrikaners and the Pacific Islanders. Both have always produced unbelievable athletes and a disproportionate number of really good international rugby players. Just think about how competitive Samoa, Tonga and Fiji are with such small populations. Their players are easily the most commonly acquired by professional teams around the world. It is the same with South Africans, who have so many players in Scotland, Ireland, England, France, and now even Japan.

Most of those players abroad are Afrikaners, and that is largely down to their physicality and size, which has always been a part of South African rugby's DNA. But it is also due to their speed. A lot of the descendants of English, Irish, Scottish and Welsh immigrants to South

Africa are big, physically imposing guys, but they aren't necessarily quick. If someone is fast, he is usually slight and less powerful.

I'll use the examples of Theuns Stofberg and Os du Randt. They weighed between 120 and 135 kg and ran the 100 metres in just over 11 seconds. That's very quick. Then look at Jonah Lomu, who ran the 100 metres in well under 11 seconds and weighed 120 kg. When it comes to rugby, players of that incredible athletic make-up are so often either Afrikaners or from the Pacific Islands.

From the 1950s right through until the 1990s, rugby was a sport that every Afrikaans father in South Africa wanted his son to play. I am told that a father in the Afrikaner community would give his young son a Bible for one hand and a rugby ball for the other. Religion and rugby were two incredibly strong elements of the culture.

The love of rugby was obsessive and the goal of playing for the Springboks was all-encompassing for so many children and their parents. The English, meanwhile, were cricket-mad, and nowhere near as obsessed with rugby to the exclusion of everything else. If you look at the famous national South African cricket side of the 1960s, for example, you will see very few Afrikaans names.

Many of the Afrikaners were farmers, and there was an enjoyment in dominating rugby opponents stemming from the physical nature of ploughing fields, operating heavy machinery and working the land. That physicality has always been a key attribute of any Springbok team, and it still is. If you dominate physically and your pack is more powerful than the opposition's, then half the battle is won. That is the South African way. As Doc Danie Craven famously said: 'Pick your tight head prop first, and then your backup tight head prop second, and pick your third-choice tight head third, then worry about the rest of your team.'

The ability to dominate physically was vital to the way South Africa played, and an example of that going wrong was in the 1974 British & Irish Lions tour. The Lions understood that if they could match the Springboks physically and compete with their pack of forwards, their backline was going to be good enough to win.

The Lions got stuck in everywhere they could and their forwards dominated South Africa. Emotionally, that was a very difficult time for the Springboks, who had never had their pack bullied in that way. The 1974 tour perfectly illustrated how much the Boks relied on physicality, and how badly things could go wrong when they didn't have it.

When the Springboks played in their first Rugby World Cup in 1995, their physicality, defence and mental strength immediately became internationally recognised as being vital in the tournament, which essentially comes down to knockout rugby.

The ability to dominate a scrum and a driving maul allows the rest of the game to fall into place, and if those facets are working, the No. 9 and No. 10 have time and they can bring the centres into the game more. At the heart of all this is the incredible physicality that is so distinctively South African. Things in this game are always evolving, but that has remained constant when it comes to the Boks, who play directly to their strengths.

The skills of the backline players come into play once the Boks get quick, front-foot ball or there is a turnover or counterattacking opportunity. That has always been the case at international level and provincial level, with the Currie Cup providing some of the most physically intense battles the game has seen over the years. That is such a key area of South African rugby, more so than for any other country.

The next reason the Boks have found so much success at World Cups? Kicking. South Africa have almost always fielded kicking fly halves rather than running fly halves at World Cups. The No. 10s who have been lauded in the press are people such as Gerald Bosch, Naas Botha, Joel Stransky, Jannie de Beer and Morné Steyn.

The Springboks will most often pick a fly half based on his kicking and his ability to be a territorial general. It has to be someone who controls the game with his boot, whereas New Zealand and France often pick a fly half as their attacking spark, someone to pass and create opportunities. For those countries, the scrum half is often the guy tasked with arranging the forwards and marshalling the troops, deciding whether to kick, pass or keep it with the forwards.

So many French captains over the years have been scrum halves – the 'little generals' who control the pack of forwards. In South Africa, the No. 9 has generally been a link between the forwards and the backs, though that has changed in recent years with the increased box-kicking from Fourie du Preez through to Faf de Klerk.

Drop goals have also played a significant part in winning World Cups over the years, so the fact that South Africa have historically had kicking fly halves has been a massive advantage. When matches at the business end of the competition are evenly poised, having a fly half who can kick a drop goal is always a wonderful option that not all teams have.

It was only when Dan Carter came along that New Zealand had a fly half who could do everything, accommodating their running ambitions as well as a kicking game. He showed the power of that combination in New Zealand's superb 2015 semifinal win over the Springboks. Carter, who kicked a drop goal that day, was ultimately the difference between the sides.

The fly half is always the guy who needs to take the key drop goal decision, and over the years the Springboks have generally been better placed than most when it comes to having No. 10s who can kick three valuable points with a World Cup hanging in the balance.

Another key element in South Africa's sustained World Cup success is that the Springbok game plan has always been based around maintaining a low error rate and giving away fewer penalties than the opposition. That allows the Boks to play for territorial dominance and to build a score – 3-0, 6-0, 9-0 – off the tee.

That game plan is something the Boks have used pretty much everywhere and under every coach, but it is also the perfect method to employ at a World Cup. Expansive tactics have not won World Cups in the professional era; instead, winners of the tournament have had the ability to defend, play for territory, kick goals, and build and maintain leads.

The Springboks will always be strong at a World Cup because playing that kind of tournament, knockout rugby, is already part of their DNA. Even when there are poor selections or a bit of unhappiness between players and the coach, the Springboks go into a World Cup with a good chance because the brand of rugby that has historically resulted in success at the tournament is part of their make-up.

Even now, in 2023, so much of the Springbok style is down to physicality. South Africans would rather run over people than run around them. That is still a prerequisite for a Springbok forward, even though the game has evolved and there are now Boks throughout the side who also have the ability to beat players with their feet.

Thankfully the game is no longer exclusively for Afrikaners, but even though the Springboks today are a fully integrated, inclusive, representative group of players, the legacy of being physically dominant remains.

When rugby was played predominantly by Afrikaners, it didn't take much more than steamrolling through an opposition tackler to earn the respect of those around you. It's very different now; the game is far more intricate, and reliant on a variety of skills and abilities, but the imperative for the Springboks to be more physical than anybody else absolutely remains. The Springboks will always prioritise players who are incredibly strong defensively and who don't mind running over someone, and that doesn't apply only to the forwards.

If you look at centre André Esterhuizen, for example, he would be the first choice No. 12 for any international team in the northern hemisphere, maybe even the world. But he cannot make the Springbok starting side, and that is indicative of the depth of physicality and strength the Springboks have at their disposal. Other nations simply don't have guys who are 1.93 metres and 118 kg, and who can run as hard and fast as Esterhuizen does. They don't produce them.

Even when the Springboks lose, the opposition leave the match knowing they have been in an epic battle, and that has always been the South African way. Whenever the Boks play, there is a physicality on defence and in ball-carrying that is direct, confrontational and absolutely fearless.

In 2019, Rassie Erasmus came up with an approach to the game that would limit errors. The Boks basically played three phases at a time, and if they didn't get any momentum from them they would kick a contestable ball. They used that tactic a lot and almost ignored backline play unless they won a turnover or there was a really poor kick on them.

There were never complaints from the backline players that they weren't getting the ball. There was a cultural discipline there and a deeper understanding that South Africans play their rugby in a uniquely South African way: to their strengths and doing what it takes to win. They follow and believe in that game plan.

That is why the Springboks are always so effective at the World Cup. It might be simplistic, but they follow it to a T. It's when South African teams are confused about what type of game plan to play that they are easier to beat. When there is absolute clarity in what they need to do, beating the Springboks is incredibly difficult.

If I had to think of a South African team that perhaps should have gone further at a World Cup, and maybe even have won, it would be the Springboks of 2011. The bulk of that team had won the 2007 edition and there was a great opportunity for back-to-back championships. They had beaten the All Blacks three times in a row in 2009, had beaten the British & Irish Lions, and were a very experienced group of quality players.

I understand that Rassie, who was a consultant on that trip, mentioned to the team before the quarterfinal against Australia that they might consider a drop goal strategy, because you never know when you might need it. The answer from the leadership group under coach Peter de Villiers was that they didn't need one and that they were good enough to smash the Wallabies without it. They probably regretted that decision after the game.

A lot of the blame for what happened that day went to referee Bryce Lawrence. That was understandable because there were so many instances where he didn't give the Springboks penalties they deserved, but that happens sometimes. In those moments, the players have to take responsibility for scoring points, and if no penalties were coming and it was difficult to score tries, how else were they going to get the scoreboard moving?

The tournament certainly wasn't disastrous and the Boks rightly considered themselves bitterly unlucky to lose the quarterfinal 11-9 in Wellington, but I felt it was an example of a Springbok team perhaps not playing to their strengths when the stakes were at their highest.

The Boks have a history of drop goals working for them at World Cups, and it could really have helped them in that match. One drop goal was slotted by fly half Morné Steyn that night to give the Springboks the lead at 60 minutes, and I can't help but wonder what the result would have been had they tried one or two more when nothing else was working for them. A drop was attempted late in the match by Pat Lambie, who was playing fullback, but Steyn was one of the best kickers in the world at the time, and he would have surely knocked over a few more points had that been the game plan.

When I think of all the Springbok sides who have gone to World Cups over the years, that is the one around which I feel there has been the biggest regret. Going into this World Cup in 2023, having a drop goal strategy will be key for South Africa, but no stone is ever left unturned when it comes to Rassie and Jacques Nienaber, and I have no doubt they will have one.

Every player who dons a Springbok jersey is fully aware of the responsibility they have. It is incredibly important to understand the magnitude of what it means to be involved in this side, particularly when it comes to travelling to a World Cup. The South African players have always been aware of that enormity.

Edward Griffiths shared a story with me after the

World Cup final in 2019 in Yokohama. The Springboks had won, and he went into the English changing room expecting them to be absolutely mortified by the 32-12 drubbing. Instead, he was greeted by routine conversation.

'What are you up to next Saturday? Are you back with Saracens?' he heard one English player say.

'Nah, they've given me the week off,' the teammate replied.

There was no introspection and there didn't appear to be a gut-wrenching feeling that they had just let the whole of England down. I can't ever imagine a Springbok team that had been knocked out of a World Cup engaging in general chitchat in the minutes after the game. They would not be anything other than crushed.

There is such a massive sense of responsibility to your country when you're representing them at a World Cup, and South Africans have always understood that. There is an acceptance that this means everything, and I'm not certain every other country can say that.

Even in the lows of Rudolf Straeuli's time, when the Boks struggled at the 2003 World Cup, the team still came out and played as hard as they could. Sometimes they went a bit too far, and there were yellow and red cards throughout that period with Corné Krige as captain.

Discipline was a problem but it also confirmed without a shadow of a doubt that these guys were giving it their all. Even in those tough times, playing for the Springboks still meant the world to the players, and they were desperate to make it work.

An obsessive focus on success and winning is inherent in South Africa's rugby culture. The team get so much heat from the media when they are not performing well, but are held up and praised as heroes when they deliver the goods. It is completely out of balance because this is only a game, but that is how much Springbok rugby means to the fans.

If a Springbok player loses in a humiliating fashion, he doesn't even want to leave his house. He wants to lock himself up for two weeks until people have forgotten about what happened. No matter what state the team might be in, when the Springboks are at a World Cup and the players who have that special green jersey on, they know the ramifications of not giving it their best.

When you take all of this into account, understanding the dominance of the Springboks at the Rugby World Cup becomes a little easier. Make no mistake, though: France 2023 promises to be potentially their greatest test yet.

3
The Springboks in 2023
... tweaking the winning recipe

Whenever the Springboks play at a Rugby World Cup, they have a massive target on their backs because of who they are. This time, that target will be even more visible given their status as defending champions.

The Springboks have never won back-to-back Webb Ellis Cups, and no team has won the tournament four times. That is the history at stake for the South Africans in France this year, and again they will take on the challenge under the leadership of Rassie Erasmus and Jacques Nienaber.

The two men took over Springbok rugby in 2018 when the team were at their lowest ebb after two difficult years under Allister Coetzee. Nienaber has confirmed that the 2023 World Cup will be his final chapter with the Springboks, and he is off to Irish club Leinster from next year. However, his contribution with Erasmus to Bok rugby has been immense.

In 2019, the Springboks arrived at the World Cup in Japan very much under the radar. Their four-year cycle had been severely disrupted by Coetzee's sacking, which left Erasmus and Nienaber with just 18 months to prepare for the tournament.

Results had been poor during that period, and even though the Boks had shown some good form heading into the World Cup, a tournament-opening 23-13 loss to New Zealand in Yokohama suggested they were not ready to challenge for the title.

Internally, though, Rassie had the team very well prepared and they had a clear, simplified game plan in their minds. They were going to play a power game with an emphasis on scrum penalties, maul penalties and territorial dominance through kicking.

The Boks were prepared to attack off turnover ball, but they were not going to take any risks at all in their half because the laws at that time made it clear to Rassie and Jacques, through an analysis of the stats, that the longer you held onto the ball in phase play, the more likely you were to give away a penalty or concede a turnover try.

Rassie wanted to eliminate that completely, and the game plan worked incredibly well after the New

Zealand loss. Wales in the semifinal were a huge challenge because they played the same style as South Africa, but in the group stages and in the quarterfinal against Japan, that simple, low-risk approach worked perfectly.

The Boks were conservative. They took driving mauls off almost every line-out, they double-shoved every scrum and they always looked to slow the game down. The Springboks wore Japan to the ground in the quarterfinal, winning 26-3 as the romantic fairy tale of the host nation took its last breath.

In the final, England tried to play a fast, offloading game but the Springbok pack and defence absolutely hammered them. Throughout the tournament, the Springboks had received criticism from supporters back in South Africa who wanted them to play more expansively. The relentless box-kicking of Faf de Klerk was a particular source of frustration, but none of that mattered when the Boks were crowned world champions and a nation celebrated.

On that famous day, 2 November 2019, the Springboks also surprised many by showing glimpses of another side to the team, and the tries scored by Makazole Mapimpi and Cheslin Kolbe were brilliant moments of attacking enterprise.

In terms of personnel, there has been very little turnover for the Springboks between 2019 and now. The likes of Schalk Brits, Francois Louw and Tendai

Mtawarira have moved on but the core of the 2023 Springboks will enter the tournament as World Cup winners, having done the business in Japan four years ago.

So, how have Rassie and Jacques freshened those players up? What has been done to bring them into this World Cup with another clear plan for how to beat the likes of Ireland, France and New Zealand? The Springboks will have to face two of those three sides before the semifinals, so it will be a huge challenge.

The performance from the Springboks during the British & Irish Lions' tour to South Africa in 2021 was superb, even though it took place under circumstances brought about by the Covid-19 pandemic. Covid meant the team had not played together consistently since the World Cup in 2019, with SA Rugby having decided against playing in the 2020 Rugby Championship.

It was to be expected, but the Springboks did not perform well in the first Lions Test, going down 22-17. They were much better in the second match, winning 27-9. Then they rolled up their sleeves, and through a display of sheer determination and grit they found a way to win the third Test 19-16 and secure a famous 2-1 series win.

To take that series, with all three Tests played at a hauntingly empty Cape Town Stadium, was a massive achievement and another hugely significant step in the players becoming a tightknit unit after their heroics in Japan.

These players under Rassie and Jacques have achieved everything there is to achieve in international rugby. With Mzwandile Stick and Deon Davids also still involved in the coaching setup, and with the core group of players still operating, there is clear continuity within the camp. There is a strong belief among the players that their coaching staff will give them the tools to beat any team they come up against, and that is exactly what happened in the Lions series.

When Rassie put himself out there after the first Test and the infamous 62-minute video in which he criticised Australian referee Nic Berry went public, it was seen as him being prepared to sacrifice himself for the benefit of the team. That made a huge statement to the players, and they trusted him implicitly and supported him wholeheartedly.

There is an understanding in the playing group that Rassie and Jacques will do anything and everything to give them the best chance of winning a Test match, and the team respond accordingly.

After the Lions series, with Rassie serving his nine-month World Rugby ban and Jacques coaching the side, 2022 became a year that saw the Springboks trying a few things and providing a testing ground for new players.

We saw the reintroduction of Damian Willemse – at fullback, fly half and centre – after he had been one of the form players in the Stormers' triumphant United Rugby Championship (URC) campaign in 2021/22. Willemse – brilliant again for the Stormers in 2022/23 as they finished runners-up in the URC – has come through and looks set to take the place of Frans Steyn as a multi-talented Springbok who can play in numerous positions, either off the bench or in the starting lineup.

There was also an opportunity for ever-improving Stormers fly half Manie Libbok to get a couple of Test caps, and we saw the explosive introductions of Canan Moodie and Kurt-Lee Arendse. Injuries to guys such as Handré Pollard, Cheslin Kolbe and Lukhanyo Am allowed Nienaber to give these players their chance, and they provided an injection of something new and exciting. There was still the feeling of the Boks cutting and pasting their World Cup-winning recipe, but there were also signs of something fresh unfolding.

The Springboks won eight of their 13 Test matches in 2022 for a 61.5 per cent win ratio, and even though those results might not be acceptable to the world champions, the performance of the team was always competitive and they never lost by a heavy margin (35-23 to the All Blacks at Ellis Park was the biggest). After 2022, the team will still feel that with a fair refereeing performance, they can beat anyone.

I am convinced the Springboks were made to pay for the backlash that followed the Rassie video. I don't think they always got a fair crack of the whip last year, and they lost a few games that they could and should have won with slightly fairer, more objective refereeing.

Whether you blame Rassie or the referees for that outcome, nothing can be done about it now. But the point is that the players themselves know they are perfectly capable of beating Ireland and France away from home and, by association, anybody else.

The Springboks cleaned up England in their final match of the year, winning 27-13 at Twickenham, and they thrashed Italy 63-21 in Genoa, something no other side in the Six Nations could do. The Boks know they are good enough to beat New Zealand when they get it right, as they did in Nelspruit (26-10), so from that point of view it was a productive year.

The Springboks certainly won't have lost any self-belief and there has been no indication that they have fallen off the cliff since 2019, as has been the case with England.

From a tactical and technical perspective, 2022 also showed us that the Springboks have evolved. Teams are now aware of the South African kicking game and they are trying to counter it either by kicking long themselves or by improving in their aerial contests.

There was a strong feeling after 2019 that the Boks were becoming predictable and one-dimensional, and it left opposition sides preparing almost exclusively for that approach, believing the Boks had nothing else to turn to.

In 2022, and partly because of sides kicking at them for so long, the Springboks were given free rein and time to attack from deep. Willie le Roux was brilliant in this space, and with guys such as Kolbe, Arendse and Moodie – all exceptionally exciting and attack-minded – left the Springboks flexing an entirely different muscle from the one the world was used to seeing.

If there was space, and if the opposition's forwards had been slightly isolated, the Springboks would suddenly have a crack at it, and the fact that they did it so well gave so much more variety to the South African game plan. Sides can no longer simply kick at the Springboks and expect to get the ball back, because there is now the real possibility of being met by a dangerous counter-attack. It was a tactic that proved particularly effective for the Springboks on their end-of-year tour to Europe, where one might traditionally expect a kick-heavy approach.

There is now an attacking freedom about the Springboks that has also been perfectly displayed by the Stormers under John Dobson in the URC; an ability to attack off turnovers and poorly directed kicks.

It's hugely encouraging that South Africa have been promoting that style, because it means they are not simply resting on their laurels in the hope that the same blueprint will be enough to win another World Cup in 2023.

There will be a clear plan for each opponent in France – what Scotland bring will be different from what Ireland bring, for example – but I believe the Boks now have more weapons in their arsenal to take on those challenges.

World Cups are won on a dominant pack of forwards, a halfback pair who kick for territory, winning and forcing penalties through set pieces, and an unbreakable defence. Those are the key pillars the Springboks have. They had them in 2019, they have them now, and they consider themselves better in those areas than anyone else in the world. The Boks will not move away from that fundamental blueprint, and nor should they.

No matter how many people ask, 'Why don't we play like New Zealand and run the ball from everywhere?', it is not in South Africa's DNA. The Springboks succeed by dominating physically, as opposed to running around defenders, and that will very much be the case again in 2023. The difference this time, though, is that the Boks are about more than that now. Over the past four years, a culture of fast, skilful, precise and dangerous counter-attacking has been cultivated, and that is imperative to their success.

There is already a lot of variety in Ireland's game, for example. They are not a team you can bracket as being any one thing – a mauling, kicking or forwards-first outfit. Ireland continually vary the way they play, backing what they believe to be the best approach at that moment.

If you are going to win tournament-deciding World Cup matches, you must have a bit of that variety, especially when your competitors have identified how to close the gap on whatever worked for you previously. Seeing the Springboks develop that side of their attack has been extremely positive, and it sets them up well going into their title defence, especially considering that they will have most of the same players they had in Japan.

There will be additions – players such as Arendse simply must go to France – but there will be continuity all over the park, injuries aside. The tight five will be as strong as it was in 2019. Pedigreed, physical players will be included in the starting lineup and on the bench, where the 'Bomb Squad' will again play a major role.

Aside from 'Beast' Mtawarira, who has retired, the likes of Steven Kitshoff, Frans Malherbe, Bongi Mbonambi and Malcolm Marx are all world-class 2019 winners, while Ox Nché, Trevor Nyakane, Thomas du Toit and Vincent Koch are still involved.

The Boks have a group of locks – Eben Etzebeth, Lood de Jager, RG Snyman and Franco Mostert – who are the envy of the world, and regardless of who they field on the day, you know they will be incredibly powerful there. Marvin Orie is the latest addition, having impressed in the Stormers setup before taking his Bok chance in 2022.

In the loose forwards, there is so much quality that the question is not so much who to take to the World Cup as who to leave behind. Deon Fourie, Jasper Wiese, Elrigh Louw, Evan Roos and Kwagga Smith have all proven themselves real options, showing the depth the Boks have, which is good news given that captain Siya Kolisi is in a race against time to be fit.

At scrum half the Springboks have also bulked up, and there are now options beyond Faf de Klerk: Herschelle Jantjies, Jaden Hendrikse and Grant Williams have all been included in the setup since 2019.

At fly half, too, the Boks used to rely on Handré Pollard and Elton Jantjies but now there are the likes of Damian Willemse and Manie Libbok, who have shown they can slot in if needed. Both have grown enormously in the last two years. Libbok has been the top points scorer in the URC for back-to-back seasons, and while he couldn't get the Stormers over the line in their final against Munster in 2023, he has evolved into the complete playmaker.

At centre, André Esterhuizen is about as good as a

player can be without being the first choice for his country. In the Springbok squad, he is backup to Damian de Allende, while Lukhanyo Am at No. 13 is considered by many to be the best in the world in his position.

Then, in the outside backs, the Springboks have taken an already world-class back three and grown even more with the arrivals of Kurt-Lee Arendse and Canan Moodie.

The World Cup squad had not been announced at the time of writing this book, and there are always last-minute injuries and unforeseen circumstances. But regardless of what happens, the Springboks have quality depth absolutely everywhere.

Backing the guys who have done it before will almost certainly be the way Rassie and Jacques will go. Obviously they would like to have everyone fit for the build-up, and opportunities will be given to ensure the Boks are prepared in all departments. Players will use all the minutes available to them – at club or international level – to show they have what it takes to be backed in France.

The Springboks do, however, have a strong policy around selection, and a player must play himself out of the side before a change is made. Just because a guy is playing well for his franchise doesn't mean he jumps ahead of the incumbent. The Springbok coaches show unbelievable loyalty towards their players in this selection philosophy, but at the same time the players know there is always somebody pushing them for their place.

Willie le Roux's performance at the 2019 World Cup is the perfect example of that loyalty. He struggled during the tournament and felt the heat from the South African rugby public back home. Le Roux did not play well in the semifinal against Wales, but when calls for him to be dropped grew louder than ever, Rassie didn't even consider it. He stuck to his guns, backed his man, and Le Roux was not only superb in the final but has been superb since.

You have to work very hard to knock a player off his perch in this Springbok team, so indications are that the Boks in France will strongly resemble the group that conquered the world in 2019.

The Springboks who went to the World Cup in New Zealand in 2011 were also made up largely of the squad that won the 2007 championship in France. The obvious and major difference this time, however, is that there has been no backroom disruption. In 2007, the Springboks won with Jake White as their chief tactician, and while most of those players were involved again in 2011, the four-year cycle happened under a different coach in Peter de Villiers.

A whole new coaching group that arrived with De Villiers had a very different style from White and brought a different playing philosophy. The big players in 2011 would have wanted to win another World Cup more than anything, but they were operating in a different environment.

There will be no such concerns for the Boks in 2023. They might have evolved into a different rugby side, capable of doing different things, but all of that has happened under the same framework. There is such a clear understanding evident in this group of Springboks. They know what is expected of them on and off the field, and they understand the selection policy. The coaches are transparent with the players, telling them when they're going to start and when they aren't, and why.

A lot of these players are now based overseas, and coming back into a Springbok camp is something they always look forward to. There is also an embedded understanding of the importance of being a Springbok and what a World Cup means to the South Africans they represent, so I don't think there will be any risk of complacency.

Springbok fans have the right to feel optimistic about a title defence in 2023. For most competing nations, the last four years have been about starting again and rebuilding, with new leadership, towards France. Not the Springboks. Preparations for this moment started all the way back in 2018.

And while 2019 was a beautiful bonus, winning the 2023 World Cup has always been the objective for Erasmus and Nienaber. Part of that process has been ensuring that the Bok class of 2023 are stronger than the Bok class of 2019, and having looked at developments over the last couple of years, I think they are.

The Springboks are as primed as they can be to do it all over again.

4
North vs South
... closing the gap

The draw for the 2023 Rugby World Cup has been a major talking point in the build-up to the tournament, and with good reason. Because of where the teams were seeded and ranked when the draw was conducted all the way back in December 2020, we now have half of the draw saturated with the best teams in the world and the teams in the other half facing a far less daunting ride to the semifinals.

The teams ranked one to five – Ireland, New Zealand, South Africa, France and Scotland (before the 2023 Rugby World Cup)– are all on one side of the draw, while the sides ranked six to nine – Australia, England, Wales and Argentina – are on the other. It is an unfortunate situation because you want the best sides in the world meeting at the business end of the tournament, not the beginning. But it does make for a very intriguing path to the final.

Pool A and Pool B are on a collision course for the quarterfinals, which makes for some blockbuster fixtures early in the tournament. Ireland, South Africa and Scotland are in Pool B, while hosts France and New Zealand are in Pool A.

The reward for the Springboks potentially topping their pool would be a quarterfinal against either New Zealand or France. It is the most unenviable draw for the defending champions and it makes this World Cup difficult to predict.

Even if you disregard the draw, the 2023 World Cup has a different feeling to it. Much of that has to do with the likes of France and Ireland believing this is finally their time to land the Webb Ellis Cup, and recent form suggests they have plenty of reason to be optimistic.

Anyone who has followed rugby closely over the last four years has seen how southern hemisphere dominance of the sport has been slowly eroded by the northern hemisphere. This has happened for several reasons, and sharing coaches is one of them.

Over the years, a lot of coaches from the southern hemisphere (particularly New Zealand and Australia) have moved overseas and continued their careers there. It might have been because they missed out on their own national team job – as was the case with Dave Rennie and Eddie Jones – or it could have simply been because they were offered an enticing, lucrative opportunity. Either way, it has resulted in many highly respected tactical rugby minds taking their skills abroad. This has brought an increase in the sharing of rugby intellect across borders, which has benefited the northern hemisphere sides immensely.

It wasn't that long ago that your semifinal bankers at the start of a World Cup were New Zealand, Australia and South Africa, and it was a case of which northern hemisphere side would join them in the final four. Those days are now over, and the northern hemisphere sides are a force to be reckoned with.

This is not only due to the coaching drain but also to the mobility of players, and this is particularly true of South Africa. So many players, for whatever reason, have sought to further their careers in Europe. In many cases, it is the strength of the euro or the pound that nudges a player to head north, but the decision becomes even easier if he believes he doesn't stand a realistic chance of Springbok selection.

If a player is with a professional South African franchise and not on the national radar, a move overseas becomes a good option for him to secure financial stability while also having a crack at becoming a Test contender for a country where there could be less competition for a position.

Rugby careers are short and players need to maximise their earning potential, but this reality has contributed towards a globalisation of the game that has made sides such as Scotland, Ireland and France far more competitive, both domestically and in the Test arena.

It's affected South Africa most, but Australia and New Zealand have also lost players to the North. Nick Evans, who was capped by the All Blacks in 2004, is the perfect example. He was a very promising young fly half, but with Dan Carter around he saw his opportunities would be extremely limited. He packed his bags, headed to England and became one of the most successful players in the Premiership. His decade-long career with Harlequins made him one of the club's all-time greats.

It used to be a case of players and coaches heading to Europe as retirement approached, but more and more we are seeing them making the move in their prime. A combination of coaches and players from the southern hemisphere moving their skills into Europe has strengthened the playing pool but also the overall intellectual property of northern hemisphere rugby, and the benefits of that are being seen now at a national level.

There is no question that the physicality, speed and aggressive defence of the southern hemisphere nations have historically been superior to those of the northern hemisphere, though one could argue that the World Cup-winning England side of 2003 had a very southern hemisphere edge to it. They had players who were imposing and prepared to get stuck in, such as captain Martin Johnson and Lawrence Dallaglio. Matt Dawson was a chirpy scrum half you might have associated with being Australian, they had a kicking fly half in Jonny Wilkinson, a pack of forwards who could dominate scrums, strong ball carriers and a real physicality on both defence and attack.

At every other World Cup, though, there has been a very clear southern hemisphere dominance. Until now. Suddenly, the defending champions face major threats to their title from all over the globe. Let's look at the potential title contenders who will be challenging for South Africa's crown, examining their progress over recent years.

Ireland

A lot of thought has gone into how Ireland have managed their professional game, and they have understood the need to keep their best players in the country. There is even a tax incentive for those who stay. Players who devote their entire professional careers to playing in Ireland can recover a huge amount of tax when they eventually hang up their boots, simply by not going overseas to play in France, Japan or anywhere else. For a small country such as Ireland, it's such a smart way of holding onto their talent. It has seen guys such as

Brian O'Driscoll and Johnny Sexton spend their entire careers within their own system.

Ireland were also one of the first countries to look at player workload and at how many games each player should be playing per season. They started working with their franchise heads and asking them to hold back on selecting their internationals for every club match. Their player management has been excellent, and resting key personnel gave opportunities to other players during the regular domestic season. In turn, this grew the talent pool and gave them a depth they might otherwise not have had. You see Leinster benefiting from that immensely these days, with quality coming through all the time, and ultimately it has resulted in stronger talent pushing up into the national side.

Ireland reached No. 1 in the world building up to the 2023 World Cup, and one of the reasons is the continuity factor that exists between the franchise coaches and the international coaches under high performance director David Nucifora, who does a superb job.

Ireland don't have the best tight head prop, loose head prop, lock or ball-carrying forward in the world, but they have incredible consistency in selection and coaching strategy, which makes a huge difference. When the players go up from club level – Leinster, Munster, Ulster or Connacht – to the national side, they are not starting from scratch. There is already a huge amount of understanding there, which becomes crucial in how they approach their Test rugby. Because of that alignment, Ireland's players are all on the same page long before they arrive at a World Cup or even at a national camp.

England have suffered because of exactly this. There, the Rugby Football Union does not have control over the domestic system. Clubs are independent and are owned by individuals or consortiums, and there is often a bit of disagreement as to who pays the salary of an international player if he is unavailable for club games. The national coach might want to take his players abroad for a camp ahead of the Six Nations, for example, and that can also become a difficult negotiation between club and country.

Ireland have no such issues. Of all the sides at Rugby World Cup 2023, they have displayed the best teamwork. The coordination, organisation and understanding that starts at the top and filters down to the bottom of their structures is unrivalled. It is no coincidence that Ireland finished with three teams in the top five on the URC log in 2022/23, with Munster, the lowest-ranked of those, going on to win the competition when they downed the defending champion Stormers in Cape Town.

Ireland have now also won a Grand Slam in the Six Nations, which is an outstanding achievement, and they beat New Zealand 2-1 in a series away from home in 2022. Those are returns that nobody should be taking lightly. They are an incredibly strong outfit and will pose a real threat to the Springboks in their pool clash at Stade de France on 23 September.

New Zealand

The All Blacks were arguably at their lowest point in 20 years after that Ireland series. They had lost at home to Argentina and there were a lot of questions hovering around head coach Ian Foster and his staff. The team were playing a brand of rugby devoid of any forward dominance or carriers, they were not strong at set piece and seemed almost totally dependent on individual skill. They were basically falling apart.

So, Ireland's series win in New Zealand does need to be put into perspective, given the way the All Blacks were playing at the time. Since Jason Ryan joined the national team as forwards coach from the Crusaders midway through last year, however, there has been a massive improvement and a complete change in how they are playing.

The All Blacks enter this World Cup in almost foreign territory given the struggles they have had, performance-wise, in the build-up to the tournament. Foster had been their assistant coach for two full World Cup cycles from 2012 to 2019, and during that time he operated as a backline coach, promoting expansive play and attack. The head coach over that period, Steve Hansen, was also a backline player in his day, so there was no forward coach in the All Black setup with any proper authority. Foster was named head coach after the 2019 World Cup but things have not been easy for him.

When the All Blacks had big guys such as Jerome Kaino, Brodie Retallick and Sam Whitelock, they could play their backline game despite not having a forwards-minded approach. When a team concentrates on one area of the game more than any other, though, some areas tend to start suffering over time.

Historically, scrums in New Zealand and Australia have been a way to restart a game more than anything, but in South Africa they have been viewed as an opportunity to win a penalty. There has been a massive difference in the way these countries have approached scrummaging, and slowly but surely over the years under Foster as head coach, New Zealand lost the ability to dominate the opposition through their pack.

In August 2022, Foster was very nearly fired but held on by getting rid of two of his assistant coaches, John Plumtree and Brad Mooar. I thought that was very unfair. The responsibility lies with the head coach, and the way the side plays should not be blamed on the assistants.

Foster was fortunate to keep his job, to say the least, but the appointment of Ryan as forwards coach has really stiffened the spine of the New Zealand team. They have gone back to a Crusaders pack and are a side that now concentrate on scrummaging and mauling again. There is suddenly far more physicality in their ball-carrying and an understanding that you've got to go down the field before you go across the field. That's the big change they have made, and just in time.

The All Blacks have come back from the edge of the abyss and seem to have their house in order when it matters most. They will be very dangerous at this World Cup because people are writing them off without understanding that while they still have all those great backline players, they now have a forwards coach who is going to get them to go down the field.

New Zealand and France have been drawn in the same pool, and the tournament opener between them on 8 September could be a World Cup final given the quality and star power on offer.

France

France, the hosts in 2023 and the second-best side in the world heading into the competition, have always had a plethora of very talented players, much like South Africa. The huge difficulty has been to take different players from different clubs, with different identities, and put them together in a national team of the quality, organisation and structure of the type you might see from Ireland, for example.

Where France took a huge leap forward in that regard – and made the right choice – was in the appointment of Fabien Galthié as head coach in 2020. Fabien is a personal friend of mine and he captained my Stade Français team when I coached there in 2003. He went to four World Cups as a scrum half and was recognised as the 2002 World Player of the Year.

A lot like Rassie Erasmus, he has a very astute rugby brain. Not only was he an exceptional player, but he always thought about the game deeply and still does. He recognised very quickly that there was a lack of organisation in the way France played, they depended a lot on individuals (like New Zealand), and they were horribly ill-disciplined. They were going into games full of emotion and intent and giving away 10 penalties in the first half. You simply can't win like that.

Their defence was not structured or organised, and the arrival of Englishman Shaun Edwards as defence coach immediately after the 2019 World Cup was an acknowledgement of that problem. That appointment has proved to be a masterstroke, and Edwards has come in and made the players realise that good defence is crucial to any attack. It's about trusting the person outside and inside of you, defensively. But first you need a defensive system that everyone buys into.

Edwards was the defence coach for Wales in 2019 and he did brilliantly, with Wales beating France 20-19 in the quarterfinals and coming within inches of eliminating the Springboks in the semifinals. He is extremely highly rated, so I think France pulled a rabbit out of the hat by getting him to join them for the four-year cycle leading into 2023.

Edwards is a calculated, meticulous and committed coach who gets all his players on the same page, and

France's defence has been a huge factor in the team's overall improvement since 2019. They have also become a far more disciplined outfit, a direct result of the defensive structure that has transformed the way they operate on match day.

In Galthié, France have a coach who has also been a very careful selector. He understands that rugby games are not necessarily won through brilliant backline players. He saw in 2019 how much success South Africa enjoyed from the 'Bomb Squad' and having a big pack of forwards who could get them across the advantage line and in a position where they could control the game.

When France won the Six Nations in 2022, they kicked more than anyone and used their physicality to win big matches, most noticeably against Ireland. In the Six Nations in 2023, while they didn't start well, their 53-10 win over England at Twickenham in round five was the game that showed exactly how capable they are.

On their day, when they get everything right, France are as dangerous as any other side in the game, all over the park. You simply cannot rule them out at their home World Cup. They have a head coach who is intelligent and consistent in selection, a defence coach who has transformed their game, a captain in Antoine Dupont who is without doubt the best scrum half in the world, and a substitutes bench that is as powerful as that of the Springboks.

There is a structure to French rugby now that we

would never have spoken about four years ago. I always considered them an exciting side, capable of breaking a game open, but they are a different prospect entirely in 2023.

Scotland

Scotland have been superb in this World Cup cycle and have claimed huge scalps along the way. They have beaten the likes of Australia and England and have earned the respect of the international rugby community.

For them to be pooled alongside Ireland and South Africa at the World Cup is incredibly unlucky, given the growth they have shown over the last four years. If Scotland were in a pool with Australia or England, or both, I would back them to beat those sides, finish top and set off for the tournament knockouts.

They are a team that has benefited hugely from southern hemisphere players, particularly South Africans, who have become Scotsmen after three years in the country, such as WP Nel, Pierre Schoeman, Duhan van der Merwe, Kyle Steyn, Boan Venter, Huw Jones and Sione Tuipulotu. There are a lot of players from outside Scotland's borders in the Scottish setup, but they have been open about the fact that they have to be competitive.

In order to grow the game in Scotland, they need their national side to do well, and this has seen them open the door and actively seek quality players. It is difficult to fault them for that. I believe that living in a country for three years should not be enough time to qualify to play for the national side, but the proactivity of the Scottish rugby administrators must be applauded.

The Finn Russell factor is also one that opposition sides can never ignore. He could have an absolute blinder on the day and Scotland could beat Ireland or the Springboks and throw Pool B wide open. They have that ability. When Russell is on the ball, he makes things happen, and Scotland are not a side that can be bullied up front any more. Their backline is also a lot stronger, physically, than one might be used to, and it all points towards a side capable of challenging the best in the world.

That is precisely what is so exciting about this World Cup: games in that pool – where Ireland, South Africa and Scotland will do battle – are likely to be almost more exciting than a quarterfinal. Those matches will be absolute crackers, and when the group stages are over one of the best sides in the world will not have made the World Cup knockouts. It really is the stereotypical 'group of death', and while the draw might be unfair it also provides an intriguing set of circumstances that directly affects the Springboks.

Because of the draw, two of the top four sides in the world will not make the semifinals. If Scotland are eliminated in the group stages, then the quarterfinals will be Ireland/South Africa v New Zealand/France, and whichever way the cards fall it is a shame that two of those sides will be out before the semifinals.

If we accept that Scotland are the fifth-best side in the world, then the draw also ensures that by the time we reach the semifinals, three of the top five rugby nations will be out.

The rest

Of course, all of this helps the teams on the other side of the draw – Australia, Wales, Argentina and England – who are likely to clash in the quarters, barring any upsets. Of those sides, I would only really look at Australia or Argentina as threats, given how unbelievably poor Wales and England were in the 2023 Six Nations.

England cannot miraculously find a tight head prop who will suddenly compete with the likes of Steven Kitshoff, for example, and they just don't have the players to match the quality and coaching strategies of the teams they will have to face in the semifinals, if they get that far. I don't think any of these four teams will frighten France, New Zealand, South Africa or Ireland.

Australia

Australian rugby endured a traumatic year in 2022 that resulted in a late head coach change in the context of

World Cup preparation. It reminded me very much of the world of football, where if there is no immediate success you simply put someone else in there and see how he goes.

Remarkably, Eddie Jones has been given the reins despite being fired from the England job, and his seven-year stint in London shows how tough it is for any coach who goes beyond a four-year cycle with an international team. It can be very difficult to maintain standards for eight straight years, and Jones was on a slippery downward spiral with England since they played against the Springboks in the final of the 2019 World Cup and lost as favourites.

Australia appointed Jones for the freshness he will bring, with new plans and a new attitude. I believe former coach Dave Rennie did as well as he possibly could with the players he had at his disposal, and he was unlucky to lose his job. Australia don't have a big playing pool and they are struggling to find quality in key positions – from their tight five to their fly half.

Rennie was trying to play a running game but he could never settle on a decent halfback pairing, and when you go through the spine of that team, players were changing all the time. The Wallabies have no world-class players in those key positions and they do not have a world-class pack. In really tight World Cup games, you need your forwards to dominate and take control of a game, and I don't think Australia have players capable of doing that.

They will battle in that department regardless of who their coach is, but Jones has a history of bringing immediate change to a team and making an impact, even when he worked as a technical consultant with Jake White during the Springboks' victorious 2007 campaign.

He has form and a track record when it comes to World Cups, and his big advantage is being on the favourable side of the draw. The Wallabies should have enough to get through to the semifinals – they will play either England or Argentina in their quarterfinal – but I think that is as far as they can go.

Wales

All four Welsh franchises have failed to finish in the top half of the URC table for two years in a row. That about sums up Welsh rugby at present. There are all sorts of issues around players and contracts behind the scenes and within the national body, and Wales also changed their head coach in a last-ditch effort to salvage something from what has been a near-disastrous World Cup cycle.

Warren Gatland, a well-known face in Welsh rugby, has replaced Wayne Pivac as head coach. Gatland is a trusted hand, but we saw no dramatic improvements in the Six Nations this year. Wales finished second bottom with just one victory, and Pivac would surely have achieved at least the same results if he had stayed on.

When you have an ageing team with young players who don't yet have the experience, combined with all the background problems of players considering leaving Wales for other opportunities, it would be very difficult for any coach to get a good performance out of the national side. Gatland will continue to play his 'Warrenball' type of rugby, which is about limited risk and similar to what South Africa played in the 2019 World Cup, but it is hard to see them going far in France.

Given how far they have slipped in the last three years, Wales are easily the biggest beneficiaries of the dreaded draw. They will also play either England or Argentina in the quarterfinals, and they will have a chance there regardless of the opposition. But they cannot be considered capable of achieving much more than that.

England

The decision to sack Eddie Jones in December 2022 and bring in the highly rated Steve Borthwick was a huge call after the work Jones had put in with England for seven years. Jones had taken England so very close to a World Cup title in 2019 – falling to the Springboks in the final – and around that time England were considered the best side in the world by many critics and pundits.

Things went downhill after that, though, and Jones

made numerous changes to backroom coaches and personnel. By the time they won two out of five in the 2022 Six Nations, the frustration in English rugby was bubbling, and when they won one out of four at home in November, Jones's fate was sealed. His last Test in charge was a 27-13 loss to the Springboks at Twickenham, while there was also a 30-29 home loss to Argentina a few weeks earlier.

In hindsight, England probably should have gone with a new coach in 2020 even though they were runners-up in 2019. It would have been a very brave decision, but it would have given a new coach a full four-year cycle to make his mark with a new voice and vision. Instead, what has happened feels rushed and last-minute.

Borthwick is as English as they come, and that will have worked in his favour. He captained his country as a player, won the Premiership with Leicester as a coach and is a meticulous planner and an exceptional rugby mind. The players know what Borthwick is about, and his background as a forward means he values that element of the game and will try to bring England back to the basics of winning the tight five battle.

I was certain Borthwick would back a kicking fly half, so it came as a massive surprise when he chose Marcus Smith in the No. 10 jersey for the Six Nations game against France this year. The 53-10 hammering England took that day surely marks one of the lowest points in their proud history, and while it showed France's ability in spades, it also illustrated just how far the 2003 world champions have fallen since 2019.

The decision to run at France was so against Borthwick's coaching philosophy, and it may have come because of the pressure from journalists and pundits who called for a more expansive game. England showed in that match that they are not ready for an All Blacks-like attack-from-anywhere approach. Their defence was also all at sea, and they didn't have a clear understanding of what the structure was supposed to be.

Those cracks were also visible when the Boks beat England at Twickenham in November 2022, and things have been in a steady state of decline for England on most fronts since.

A tremendous amount of work will have to be done to get this side ready for France 2023, but the good news for England is that the draw helps them immensely. They will fancy themselves against either Australia or Wales in the quarterfinals, and then will hope for an upset against one of France, New Zealand, South Africa, Ireland or Scotland in the semis.

But while England might have the benefit of the draw, they do not have a tight five, and I think that is what will hurt them most. If you're still putting 36-year-old Dan Cole on your bench as your replacement tight head prop in 2023 after he last featured when he was smashed by South Africa for 75 minutes in the 2019 final, that shows a massive lack of depth up front.

England just don't have the forwards to dominate any of the big guns on the other side of the draw, so it will be very difficult for them to go much further than the semifinals.

Argentina

Because of the southern hemisphere exposure they have through the Rugby Championship, Argentina continually test themselves against the best and have become a very dangerous team. They have had some superb results post-Covid, and because of the favourable draw the Pumas will believe they can go deep into the 2023 showpiece.

Argentina have now won in New Zealand for the first time, which was an extraordinary effort, and they also beat England away from home in November 2022. They have big tight forwards, a strong spine of players, and by playing against New Zealand, South Africa and Australia they have learnt how to close out games.

In Michael Cheika they have a very experienced coach who is incredibly passionate, competitive and street-smart. He also adds a lot of structure and organisation, in between all the chaos.

Out of all four of the leading teams on the 'easy' side of the draw, Argentina have the ability to put up a really good fight against New Zealand, South Africa, France, Ireland or Scotland. It would be a hard-earned victory for one of those teams against Argentina, who are improving all the time and are now a real force in world rugby.

It would be an incredible story if Argentina did make it all the way through to the final on 28 October, and they are a side that teams will be quite happy to avoid along the way given their impressive form in 2021 and 2022.

Argentina have a very good defensive structure, a strong scrum and good variety in the line-outs; and while they are physical in how they take it up, their backline also has the skill and speed to make things happen when the opportunity arises. They also have a superb goalkicker in Emiliano Boffelli, who keeps them accumulating points from anywhere inside the opponent's half.

Argentina are without doubt a side worth watching, and capable of producing a major upset along the way.

5
Destination France
... pride and passion

I was fortunate to play and coach rugby in France for a combined 11 years. I spent five years playing for a second-division side, St Claude – in the Jura region close to the eastern border with Switzerland – from 1985 to 1990, then four years in Paris with Boulogne-Billancourt, also a second-division side, until 1994.

After my time coaching the Springboks had come to an end in 2000, I went back to France and coached Stade Français from 2002 to 2004. I have a deep knowledge and appreciation for the country, both culturally and from a rugby perspective, and I've had really good experience of what the game is like there.

During my time there from 1985 to 1994, I operated as a player/coach and the rugby was largely amateur. I feel very proud to have helped both St Claude and

Boulogne-Billancourt win promotion to the French First Division, albeit in Serie B, during my time there. What a wonderful cultural experience it was!

I remember getting a call from Dugald MacDonald, who was a well-travelled South Africa and Western Province loose forward who had played in Italy and France. He told me about an opportunity at a small club, St Claude, who played in the French second division.

Their coach and captain was leaving for another club. His name was Nigel Horton, a lock who made 20 appearances for England between 1969 and 1980. Dugald told me the job came with an opportunity to run your own business, the Café le Club, which was a small bar and bistro. All the profits would go to me, and when Dugald gave me the figures, it was a lot more than I was earning in South Africa.

I was already married at the time and my wife Jane was finishing her university degree, so I decided to go over for six weeks to test the waters ... and the rest is history.

I didn't speak a word of French and had never studied it at school. I had played some rugby in Italy in 1982 and 1983, so I could speak a little bit of Italian, but French? *Pas du tout!* The first couple of weeks were very difficult. I was working behind a bar and didn't understand a word people were saying to me. This made for some interesting food and drinks orders, because they didn't speak any English and didn't understand a word I was saying either.

The English teacher at the town's school would arrive and ask me how to pronounce English words, because even she couldn't speak the language fluently. I was completely immersed in a French environment.

It took me a month or so before I was understanding French better than Italian. After two or three months, I could understand all the rugby terminology and the words used in the café regarding food and drinks, and I was starting to feel confident enough to speak French, too. Six months in, I think I was speaking quite well.

My definition of how you know when you're starting to understand a language well is when you can detect humour and sarcasm. I remember locals would come in on a Monday morning and say, 'Nick, you weren't on form on Saturday,' and I would be offended because I knew I had played well. 'I didn't play badly, I scored two tries,' I would protest, to laughter.

I had been translating everything directly from French to English and it took me a while to start understanding the differences in tone that accompanied French humour. Before long, I was teasing the locals myself in their own language. It was such an exciting journey to have as a young man, and I feel so very blessed and privileged to have been given that opportunity.

My wife and I ended up living there for nine years, and St Claude will always hold such a dear place in our hearts. Our children were both born in that little town, which holds such precious memories for us. We visit France whenever we can.

St Claude might have been a small club playing in the second tier of French rugby, but that certainly didn't change how competitive the players and supporters were. A clear tribalism exists in how the French support their teams. Rugby there is not played on a regional or provincial basis, as it is in South Africa; instead, every town has its own team.

At weekends, the town will turn out almost in its entirety to support its rugby team, and it is incredibly special. St Claude, I remember, had a population of just 13 000 during my stay there. If we won on a Saturday, the bistro would do really well, and I'd have guys coming in for coffee or drinks throughout the week and wanting to talk about the game. If we lost, however, it was a different story, and I felt it in my pocket.

The citizens of St Claude became extremely emotional about winning and losing. In one of the seasons we got through to the second division final, and I think there were around 7 500 of our fans – more than half the town's population – at the neutral venue where the match was played.

The French really do buy into a successful side, and when things are going well they are some of the best supporters in the world. It works both ways, though. French supporters will also be very critical if the side doesn't perform, and they can lose interest and simply stay away if the struggles continue.

It is exactly the same with the national side. If France are going through a rough patch, the fans will stop watching and switch channels to soccer or something else. But if the side are in a good space and performing, as they are presently, you get this massive groundswell of public opinion, affection and support behind the national team.

I remember when I was Springbok coach and we were playing against France in Paris in 1997, the crowd began by cheering for their side, but by halftime they were booing them off the field. In the second half, the crowd started supporting us and applauding the rugby we played. We won the game 52-10.

When you play against the French, you know that if you put them under pressure so that they start making mistakes, there is a good chance their fans will quickly turn on them and make it even harder for them. In some ways, it is similar to South Africa where our supporters are also hugely emotional about the fortunes of the Springboks.

Being the French coach operating in such a volatile, frantic and fickle environment is a tough gig, but Fabien Galthié has done a fantastic job and he has the support of the country going into their home World Cup.

I have such fond memories of my time in France, particularly at St Claude. I remember another occasion when we were playing a side away from home – I can't remember who – and we were far better than them.

I think the referee must have been influenced by the opposition club president or management, because we were being penalised for absolutely everything, and we ended up losing a very close game – I think it was 15-12 – despite having been comfortably better than our opponents. We had scored a couple of tries, and all their points were from penalties.

Some travelling fans had made the trip with us, and one supporter was so angry that he waited for the referee to get into his car and then chased him down the road and onto the highway. That is obviously unacceptable behaviour that would earn someone a life ban today, but it does illustrate how incredibly emotional French fans can get when things don't go their way.

Another infamous story from St Claude happened before I arrived there, though I was quickly made aware of it. A group of supporters tipped the referee's car over and rolled it down a hill after a home defeat which they felt was poorly officiated. The vehicle landed in a river!

I also remember an incident where we had about 5 000 fans at a home game and they all invaded the pitch, leading to a massive fistfight between them and the visiting supporters. Three guys were put in prison that weekend, and it didn't take long for me to realise that French fans can go in way over the top in support of their team.

It hasn't been a surprise for me to see that in games played in France, the television angles presented to the television match official (TMO) and referee are often strangely selective, or that communications between the referee and the TMO sometimes break down for no apparent reason. We have seen it in Test matches, including the one against the Springboks in November 2022 (France won 30-26), and more recently in European Champions Cup and Challenge Cup matches.

I found France very different from South Africa, where I always felt you had an opportunity to win whether you were playing at home or away. In South Africa, a game of rugby was simply between two teams and the referee would always try to be fair. In France, however, there has always been a tendency for home fans to expect that their side will win.

You would find a winning percentage of something like 80 per cent for home teams during those days. Even in defeats, you would see the worst team in the division losing by just a single score to the best team in the division, if they were playing at home. It was quite bizarre. The referee simply wouldn't allow the visitors to humiliate the home team, especially when he was getting screamed at for every decision he blew against the hosts.

It has obviously improved with the age of professionalism, but inside every French supporter is this kind of passion. The French are so loyal to their sides. If you're born in a town with a rugby club, then that is your rugby club for life. It doesn't matter where you end up, you are tied to that team forever. This translates into a very strong support base for the national team, but they will support their local team more if the national team are struggling.

If France are on a good run, though, they capture the enthusiasm and passion of the fanatics in the stands. There is something almost romantic about all of this, and it makes France a very difficult place in which to win for visiting teams.

We know from the 2019 World Cup that the Springbok management group put a ridiculous amount of work into planning their trip to Japan, mapping out every single detail. They conducted a reconaissance mission the year before the tournament, trialling different hotels in the cities they would be staying in. Everything from the quality of the kitchen service to the comfort of the beds was evaluated, and journeys between hotels, airports, railway stations and training venues were all taken into account.

I have no doubt that Rassie Erasmus, team manager

Charles Wessels and the logistics team will have done something similar for France 2023, but they can also take comfort from the fact that many of the Springboks have visited France numerous times – some are even based there – and will have a good understanding of the environment and culture.

France is an incredible country with beautiful regions, wonderful wine and amazing food. It is blessed with stunning countryside, spectacular mountains and rivers, and a great deal of farmland. Every region has its own food speciality – the Toulouse sausage, for example – and there are really special dishes that come out of every region. There is so much good food that you don't know where to start. It's a gastronomic paradise.

There is so much to take in and experience, and it is the perfect place to host a World Cup. Players from all visiting countries, regardless of their skill sets or levels of experience, will soak it all in and have a tournament they will never forget. Every other time the World Cup has been played in France, they have had to share it with another nation, and in 2023 they will have it all to themselves. This is a fully French World Cup.

It's sad for South Africa, of course, having lost out on the rights to host the 2023 edition in controversial circumstances in 2017. An independent board had told World Rugby that South Africa was the favoured choice as host but France somehow managed to sneak the vote.

It is a real pity for South Africans, who have not had

a World Cup since 1995 and absolutely deserve another one given everything the country has contributed to rugby over the last 30 years.

There were clearly political moves behind the scenes that encouraged some of the key voting blocs to support France rather than the recommended South Africa, and the way all of that unfolded was an embarrassment for World Rugby.

While that is an interesting component of this tournament, from a playing perspective it is completely irrelevant. Regardless of what happened back then, France was ultimately chosen as the host nation and this will still be a very good World Cup.

From a rugby point of view, the French are very passionate about their own team and, boy, do they dislike England! They are not on the same side of the draw as England, of course, but the crowds will ensure hostile environments every time the English play.

Weirdly, the French supporters have always been allies of the Celtic teams, so they will support Wales, Scotland and Ireland, since they have a lot of respect for those nations. They also respect the southern hemisphere players and countries, so I think they will be very warm hosts, especially outside Paris in the regions.

The capital is a tourist destination throughout the year, but in places such as Toulouse, Lyon, Marseille,

Biarritz and Toulon, players and squads will get fantastic welcomes from rugby fans keen to embrace this spectacle.

The best advice for South Africa's travelling fans will be to speak Afrikaans, Zulu or Xhosa initially, because the French will take offence if you use English and you won't be served that quickly!

France really do have a great chance of winning this tournament at home, and it will translate into electric crowds whenever they are playing. The French had a 14-match winning streak under Galthié before they eventually lost to Ireland away in the 2023 Six Nations, and there is a lot of confidence and belief in the side right now.

In fact, there will be a groundswell of support for all northern hemisphere teams, with their supporters making the short trip to France from England, Ireland, Scotland, Wales and Italy. In many ways, and because success at the competition has been so limited over the years, this is a home World Cup for all those nations. They will support each other (with the exception of the French and England!) in their battle with the southern hemisphere sides, and it will create a northern hemisphere base that will undoubtedly be a theme of the World Cup.

We will see that clearly when the Springboks take on Ireland and Scotland in their pool, while France against the All Blacks in the tournament opener is a blockbuster group game that will bring the country to a standstill. There will be as much pressure and tension in that game as there will be in the semifinals and final, because so much hangs on it in terms of finishing top or second in the pool. France will have a huge amount of support.

The good news for the visiting sides is that September and October are still largely good months, weather-wise. It will obviously be cooler in Paris and up north than in the south, but we should still expect temperatures of between 15°C and 20°C, which will not be uncomfortable. There will still be nice sunny days, especially in Biarritz, Marseille, Toulon and Toulouse. That south-west region gets really good weather late into the year.

When I was coaching Stade Français the weather was still fine in October, even in Paris. I don't think it will be particularly cold, and hopefully it won't be too wet and rainy either. In my experience, it is only in November and December that things start getting really miserable.

The weather is another area where the South Africans will have an advantage over their southern hemisphere neighbours, because they have been exposed to European conditions regularly for the last two seasons after their move to the URC. Playing in Japan in 2019, I believe, would have been a much greater challenge for the Springboks, since most of them were experiencing those foreign conditions and a completely different culture there for the first time.

The language barrier is obviously one challenge they will still have going to France, but most of the top players will have played there recently through this past season's European Champions Cup with their franchises. There are also, of course, a few Springboks who are already based in France with their clubs. The time zone is not an issue either, and the many South African supporters who travel for the tournament will feel well-supported during their stay. I can't see the fact that it is in France being a problem for them at all.

Of course the Springboks have won in France before. Jake White's perfect run at the 2007 edition of the tournament ended with South Africa celebrating their second of three World Cup triumphs to date as John Smit lifted the Webb Ellis Cup into the Paris night sky on 20 October.

The final in 2023 will take place 16 years and eight days later, on 28 October, at the same venue, and South Africans certainly have enough reason to be optimistic about the Boks producing the same result.

6
Rassie

When Allister Coetzee took the Springboks on their end-of-year tour to Europe in 2017 and they lost 38-3 to Ireland in Dublin, it was the final nail in the coffin for him, having also taken a couple of 50-pointers against the All Blacks over his two years in charge.

When Rassie Erasmus took over in 2018, with 18 months to prepare for the 2019 World Cup in Japan, he basically had the same material to work with. When you consider what he did over that period, ending with the Springboks thumping England on that famous 2 November night in Yokohama to land their third World Cup crown, it really is incredible.

Rassie transformed the Boks in every way possible, taking them from being nowhere near the top tier of international rugby to world champions. In an immediate masterstroke he made Siya Kolisi his captain, then he began with an impressive, energising home series win over England – considered the side to beat at the time in 2018. The Boks never looked back. Rassie built the competitiveness of the side so quickly that they were soon challenging, and beating, the All Blacks away from home.

By the time 2019 came around, he had secured the full confidence of his players and a South African rugby public that had experienced arguably its darkest period. Rassie and the Springboks absolutely believed they could go to the World Cup and win it, and that takes some doing when you've been asked to coach a side that have completely lost their way.

Even though the Boks lost their first game of the 2019 World Cup to New Zealand – and rather convincingly – they went under the radar, made a favourable tournament draw work for them and delivered two world-class knockout punches in the semifinal against Wales and the final against England.

Eighteen months earlier there would not have been many South Africans who believed that was possible, and Rassie has rightly been lauded for the management and coaching brilliance that proved them wrong.

I was lucky enough to be at the 2019 World Cup final, and during the awards ceremony afterwards Rassie showed that despite all the bravado, he is an incredibly humble leader. The post-match speeches from Rassie and Siya were brilliant. They shared the credit.

Rassie spoke about the opposition coaches Eddie Jones (England) and Steve Hansen (New Zealand), saying they were his inspiration in wanting to keep South Africa in the top echelon of world rugby beyond their 2019 success, and not let them slip down as they had after previous World Cup wins.

There was a moment after the final when the Boks were taking a team photo, and I saw Siya go to Rassie and beg him to come and stand with his players to document this epic moment in South African history. Rassie refused; he wouldn't do it. He believed this wasn't *his* moment, but that it belonged to his players.

You could see Siya trying to push it and convince him, but Rassie was having none of it. I thought that was superb from Rassie. We were in such a good place and the world press was all over us. Yet, in that moment, he didn't make it about himself.

Siya, too, used his time in the limelight to thank all the leaders alongside him – players such as Duane Vermeulen and Handré Pollard – for how they helped him captain the Springboks to their fairy-tale win. Siya thanked the people back home and stressed what a privilege it was to play for them, and it was just such a powerful moment.

The way the Springboks handled that win was very impressive, and they made it a moment for the entire

South African population to claim as their own. In 1995, when the Springboks won their first World Cup and SA Rugby president Louis Luyt famously said that you could never consider yourself world champions until the Springboks were part of the tournament, there was an arrogance about South African rugby that still sticks in the throats of a lot of people.

None of that was present in 2019, when the Springboks became the face of what World Cup rugby is all about.

The Covid-19 pandemic, which halted all the momentum the Springboks had built through their near-miraculous World Cup success story, was hugely damaging to the South African national cause and the global product as a whole. There were serious financial implications to not playing any rugby, and when the coronavirus threatened the 2021 British & Irish Lions tour, SA Rugby realised it would struggle to pay the unions, who pay the players, if the tour did not go ahead. It was that dire.

The result was accepting a Lions series that was unlike anything we had seen before. We have always had hordes of British supporters travelling to South Africa for the tour, which brings a huge influx of tourism spend and a camaraderie between the rival fans that is difficult to match. Suddenly, we had a situation in which all the tour matches and the three marquee Tests were played in empty stadiums.

The coaches in that series – Rassie and Warren Gatland – had to find ways to motivate their sides. Gatland had been the coach of the Welsh side that lost the 2019 World Cup semifinal to the Springboks, and Rassie had motivated his players in Japan by warning them that Wales was the one side that simply never went away. That would have been something Gatland told his Lions in 2021, and it clearly worked, because the Springboks lost the first of three Tests played at Cape Town Stadium.

By that stage Rassie was no longer head coach, having appointed Jacques Nienaber to that position, as he slipped into a full-time director of rugby role. While Nienaber's head coaching credentials were questioned initially, as he had never performed that role anywhere else, I felt this was a largely seamless move considering how closely linked Rassie and Jacques have always been in their coaching careers. It's never been one or the other, but rather a combined effort between the two that has delivered enormous success wherever they have been.

Rassie made it immediately clear that while he had other responsibilities in his role as director of rugby, the Springboks remained his priority. He wanted a flagship national team that would build on the 2019 success and solidify their position as the top side in the world. The British & Irish Lions series was a hugely important step towards achieving that, as is defending their World Cup title in France.

I believe the first Lions Test was a seminal event in Rassie's relationship with World Rugby. Until then, he had gone through the normal channels to raise his concerns over officiating, and while he had no doubt irritated the sport's governing body to an extent, it was all above board.

I'll never forget the tongue-in-cheek tackling lesson he gave André Esterhuizen after losing to England in 2018, sarcastically showing his centre how to hit the player high up on the body in a tackle after the Boks had been robbed of a win at Twickenham when Owen Farrell's high hit went unpunished.

That coaching tutorial conveniently made its way onto social media, and it would not have gone down well in the World Rugby head offices. That was Rassie making a not-so-subtle point and, while it was largely laughed off at the time, it was the first sign of what was to come when he decided he'd had enough of World Rugby's referees.

Rassie was digging away at inconsistencies in officiating and felt World Rugby was not coming back quickly enough after games with answers or solutions. So when the Springboks lost the first Test to the Lions after so many controversial calls that didn't go South Africa's way, things were about to blow up.

Gatland had said before the Test that he was upset that a South African TMO, Marius Jonker, had been appointed for the series opener, and it worked. Jonker had to make a number of big calls in that match and they all went against the Springboks.

Rassie was not happy, and days later a 62-minute video appeared on social media in which he lambasted the calls made by Australian referee Nic Berry. It was unlike anything anyone had ever seen. It was essentially Rassie in his personal capacity letting rip with a diatribe against World Rugby and the officials.

He took full responsibility, removing SA Rugby from the matter as far as he could. The video was sent to key stakeholders – players, SA Rugby management, World Rugby officials – but there was always a strong chance it would be shared. To this day, Rassie maintains the video was never meant to make its way into the public space, but I find that difficult to believe. The moment it was shared, World Rugby was shaken to its core. Rassie was incredibly scathing, taking on the sport's ruling body in a way that no other coach – however disgruntled – had done before.

Naturally, there was huge fallout, and it caused the second Test to be one of the longest in the history of the game; match officials deliberated over every major call, desperate to get them right. In the end the Springboks won comfortably, and Rassie's rant was considered another masterstroke.

The third Test was incredibly tense and tight, but with the series hanging in the balance, the Springboks found a way over the line and won it 2-1.

I would go so far as to say that had Rassie not put out that video, the Springboks would not have beaten the Lions. Its impact on the series and how it was being officiated was immense. And this, for me, sums up Rassie. He is prepared to do whatever it takes to give the South African side the best possible opportunity to win. Whatever it takes. Even if it results in him being personally fined or banned, Rassie will make it happen if it helps the Springboks win.

He was eventually banned from the sport for nine months because of the video, but if he thought it was going to give his side an edge, it was a price he was willing to pay. In the short term, it helped the Springboks win their series against the Lions. I believe that fully.

In the long term, however, there is no doubt in my mind that World Rugby bears a grudge. The other Test referees rallied around Berry, fearing that if it had happened to him, it could happen to them. What if every coach decided to go on social media after every game and publish a list of things the officials got wrong? There was a strong feeling at World Rugby that Rassie had gone too far.

During his ban, it was hardly a case of Rassie being as quiet as a mouse. Every now and again you'd see a tweet of him having fun and a few drinks, and often he took further subtle stabs at World Rugby. I didn't think that was necessarily the right way to go, because while winning the Lions series was a single battle, a war against match officials would be a long one.

I think the backlash from all of this was the reason that, in 2022, there were four or five games in which the Springboks were at the rough end of poor refereeing. There were the two against Ireland and France on the end-of-year tour, but in other games before that some really unfortunate calls went against the Boks. For a coach, decisions like that are so frustrating, and I strongly believe they were a direct result of what happened in the Lions series.

Where Rassie is exceptional, and at the same time exceptionally difficult for World Rugby to control, is that he understands better than anyone the game, its laws, and how to get his team to win. He is prepared to use any law, or any slight gap in the law, to find even the slightest advantage.

One such example is designating himself the water boy for Test matches. The rules specified that only members of the coaching staff couldn't take the field. Rassie argued that, as director of rugby, he was not technically a member of the coaching staff, and that was a loophole he used to his advantage. He does that all the time, and while it obviously irritates those in charge, his enterprise must also be acknowledged and applauded.

We learnt after the 2019 World Cup of the work Rassie had done in commissioning detailed intelligence reports about the personalities of the referees in charge of South Africa's matches at the tournament. He is obsessive about how he prepares the team, and that has never gone away. He craves detail because it enables the team to go into big matches with the clearest possible idea of what they need to do to beat their opposition.

Rassie is an outstanding strategist and coach, but beyond that he has earned the trust of his team, and I believe that is imperative if you are going to win a World Cup. The coach must have the complete faith of his players and his captain, and after what Rassie did for the Boks at the 2019 World Cup and during the British & Irish Lions series, not a single player would have a bad word to say about him.

Against the Lions, he protected his team and gave them every possible chance of winning, and the players know that. They know that very few people would have gone out on a limb for them the way Rassie did. It was really extraordinary, and when you earn trust like that, the team will listen to you.

If Rassie says, 'This is the way we're going to beat New Zealand or France,' the players will be prepared to adapt to whatever those instructions are. They will take in that information and execute to the best of their ability, because they know with absolute certainty that all he is concerned about is getting the best result for the Springboks.

In all these ways – technical, tactical, trust-building, communication, commitment – I think Rassie has been brilliant. He has the buy-in of everyone involved, the players know where they stand and how they fit in, and he has transformed the Springboks into a global powerhouse that makes the rest of the world sit up and take notice. The Boks are feared by every other nation, and that is largely down to everything Rassie has instilled since 2018.

He might call himself director of rugby now, and Nienaber might be the head coach until the end of 2023, but there is no doubt that Rassie is still heavily involved in all aspects of how the Boks are preparing for their title defence. I guarantee that he is still hands-on in the changing room with the players and coaching staff. Rassie and Jacques have always been a partnership, and I'm certain that is still very much the case.

If I have a criticism, it would be that Rassie's social media behaviour after the Lions series was a mistake. People can obviously disagree with me. They can argue that I'm just a retired coach who never won a World Cup.

Rassie called me out publicly over my criticism of him during a television show in which I aired these views, and there were many who jumped to his defence. But my view on it has never changed. You work within a system that includes your employers and World Rugby, and and in doing so you must adhere to certain protocols. If you want to change a process fundamentally, you should do it in consultation with all the other coaches. One person can't sit there and fire off sniper shots. Even though it worked against the British & Irish Lions, I don't think it has helped South Africa beyond that.

The Springboks will enter the 2023 World Cup prepared in every possible way. They will have precise plans for every opposition team, they will be motivated, they will be desperate to defend their crown, and they will be more than capable all over the park.

My only worry is that they will not have control over the referees, and that because of what has transpired in the battle between Rassie Erasmus and World Rugby since 2021, they will find themselves on the wrong end of crucial calls in huge matches when it matters most.

From that perspective, I believe it would have been better not to incense the refereeing body. Everyone is human at the end of the day, and it makes complete sense that when faced with a 50/50 call you are not going to favour the person who has humiliated you and your employers in a very public way. That is my only concern and the only reason for which I would ever criticise, and have ever criticised, Rassie. I've said this to him personally.

Because of the hangover of that Lions tour, I know there is no love lost. It's so important for the Springboks that they get on the right side of the refereeing body between now and the World Cup. We'll discuss this more in a later chapter, but I was impressed with Rassie's idea of getting Nigel Owens in as a refereeing consultant for the World Cup. It didn't work out, but it would have been an outstanding move.

Looking in that direction for a facilitator to take away the acrimony between the Boks and World Rugby was another example of Rassie's incredible attention to detail and foresight. If the Boks find someone else to fill that role and operate in a way that is accepted by World Rugby, then I think South Africa will have a better chance of winning the crucial games that would be decided by one score. When you play New Zealand, France or Ireland, it is not likely that you're going to beat them by 20 points. They are going to be tight, physical encounters, so you don't need a referee blowing against you in a key moment.

Ever since my first interactions with Rassie in the 1990s, it has been clear to me that rugby has always meant the world to him. He deserves everything that has come his way both before and after that amazing 2019 World Cup success, because he has poured his heart and soul into the game.

I always liked him as a person, and as a player he was already displaying his leadership qualities. He had incredible charisma and was very good at getting cohesion going in a team. He showed that during his time in the Super 12 with the Cats when, as captain, he essentially operated as an assistant coach.

In 1999 I offered him the Springbok captaincy, and even though he turned me down it was a decision I have never regretted. Rassie backed Gary Teichmann and he didn't want Gary to miss out on the World Cup. I think there was a bit of principle there, and I can respect that thinking.

The other reason Rassie didn't want the captaincy was because of his social life. He was a young guy who didn't feel he was mature enough to take it on. Ironically, that was a decision which showed immense maturity. But from a technical point of view, and given his ability to understand the game, he was an obvious captaincy appointment.

In my last game as Springbok coach, against Australia in Durban in the 2000 Tri-Nations, I encouraged the players to let me know if they had spotted anything I hadn't seen. Rassie came to me straight away and pointed out a defensive line-out the Wallabies used repeatedly.

He argued that in our defensive system, I was asking

him to tackle Toutai Kefu off the line-out. The problem was that the ball never went to Kefu, and Rassie showed me how he could be better used in a position where he was going for the interception with defensive backup behind him in case Kefu did get the pass. I couldn't argue with his logic and we made the change.

Twenty-five minutes into the game, it happened exactly as Rassie said it would. Australia had a line-out, the ball went to John Eales off the top then down to George Gregan, who passed behind Kefu and straight into Rassie's hands. Rassie gathered, galloped, and went diving over the line with two Australians tackling him. Remarkably, the TMO couldn't see the ball being grounded – it couldn't have been anywhere else – and didn't award the try.

We lost that game 19-18, but I will always remember that moment and how Rassie had seen a technical opportunity in the game that I, the coach, had not. I have always had tremendous respect for his knowledge, and I still do.

It was obvious, even back then, that Rassie was destined for coaching. He spent so much time after matches and training sessions studying attacking, defensive and kicking options, as well as how we could improve our set pieces. He was fascinated by it and spent hours analysing the opposition. No other player was doing that at the time.

I always knew he had the technical knowledge, but I wasn't sure he'd have the self-confidence. Rassie gave the impression of having self-confidence but I questioned how much of it he had inside, and much of that I think was as a result of his difficult background.

As a coach, when you're getting a lot of flak from left and right, having that internal belief is critical, otherwise it can be a very tough time. It can be a thankless job if your team aren't doing well, so in thinking about Rassie as a future coach I was always concerned about his ability to take criticism when things were going wrong.

In that area he has grown in leaps and bounds, and now finds ways to manage it. I think having Jacques as his head coach has helped because it removes Rassie from the day-to-day scrutiny of the media, which can be brutal. I hated it.

I still think Rassie is at his best when he's not front and centre but running things behind the scenes, as he will be doing for this World Cup. I think he still struggles with criticism to an extent, and that is one of the reasons I got a lecture from him after calling out his social media behaviour on a television show. Even a little throwaway line he felt was unfair to him, and I probably should have realised that would be the case.

Rassie has always been a complex character, but we all have our quirks. We are born and grow up with different strengths, weaknesses and traits, and none of us is perfect. But all of those varying elements of obsession and passion are what make Rassie Erasmus one of the great rugby minds of this generation.

Jacques has confirmed that he will be leaving the Springboks at the end of 2023, and while Rassie is contracted until 2025, we don't yet know what his future holds. Together, though, those two can leave secure in the knowledge that they have achieved their goal of restoring the Springboks to their rightful place in the game, regardless of what happens in France. They have rescued Bok rugby and set it up perfectly for whoever comes next.

It has been one of the great coaching partnerships of the modern era. Rassie and Jacques have stuck together through thick and thin, and the fact that on the whole they have thrived wherever they have gone is testament to their abilities. They have had success together as far back as 2005, when they won the Currie Cup at the Free State Cheetahs, and have gone on to greater heights at Western Province and the Stormers, Munster and the Boks. Wherever they have gone, trophies have followed.

Rassie, though, has always been the mastermind. He is the ultimate student of this game, and under his leadership the Springboks will always be a side capable of winning a World Cup.

7
Managing the referees

Since the first Rugby World Cup in 1987, refereeing has always been in the spotlight. As much as the players on the park are the stars of this great tournament, we have often seen decisions at key moments deciding the outcomes of games.

To give themselves the best opportunity to win, this means coaching groups and players spending serious time understanding the laws of the game and how they are officiated.

That will never be truer than in 2023, with the rules stricter than ever when it comes to high hits and head knocks. For all 20 sides competing in France, managing the referee will be crucial to their cause.

Rassie Erasmus and the Springboks were the perfect examples of this in 2019, doing all they could to gather as much intelligence as possible on the referees who would oversee their matches at the World Cup in Japan.

The Springboks prepared for every intricate detail in an effort to control every possible outcome, and ultimately it worked in their favour. South Africa had Frenchman Jérôme Garcès referee three matches – including the semifinal and final – en route to the title, and they had studied his refereeing style and even his personality traits in incredible depth.

To understand the importance of refereeing in rugby, it is first important to acknowledge the psychology behind what is an extremely difficult job. In doing so, it is impossible to ignore the impact of a home nation.

Going into a World Cup, there is always a lot of hype around one or two sides: the ones that have played well in the cycle leading up to the tournament, and the ones hosting. In 2023, those two sides are France and Ireland, both on the front foot having each won a Six Nations title in the past two years while playing a hugely impressive style of rugby that is consistent and difficult to beat.

In 1995, even though South Africa weren't the favourites, there was such feelgood energy around the Springboks. Simply from a human point of view, there was almost a collective acceptance that they deserved to do well at their own World Cup, given the historical context. They were the underdogs and the crowd favourites for neutral fans, and the international media was quick to buy into their fairy tale.

That kind of momentum directly affects referees, and I think it stems from the generalisation and acceptance that human beings want to be liked. A referee can walk onto the field certain that he is going to manage the game in an even-handed fashion, but there are influences at play that can change things.

Every decision against the home side is booed to the rafters, and every time the referee penalises the away side there is a massive cheer. It takes an incredibly strong personality to ignore that, because human nature dictates that we want to be praised rather than criticised. It's something referees must fight all the time.

In 1995, South Africa did well to get into the semifinal in which they were to play a dangerous-looking French side in Durban. Persistent rain in the build-up to the match left the field wet and muddy, and in those conditions the game was extremely tight.

The Springboks thought they had scored a try when Ruben Kruger went over the line, but it wasn't clear that he had grounded the ball. Welsh referee Derek Bevan decided to award it, giving the Boks the benefit of the doubt. There were no TMOs in those days, of course, and no way to go back and check.

The most controversial moment in that game, however, came towards the end when Abdelatif Benazzi had a crack at a try and went sliding towards the line. He might have been in possession of the ball and made the grounding, there might have been a South African hand underneath the ball, or he might have been stopped just short. There was no way to tell, and there still isn't to this day.

Standing in front of a massively vocal and passionate South African crowd at Kings Park, it would have been so difficult for Bevan to award that try, because it would have knocked the Boks out of the competition. All these years later, the fact that he didn't remains a source of pain for French rugby.

France lost the game 19-15 and have still never won a World Cup, and this story goes to show how much influence one call can have in shaping the history of the game. It wasn't that it was the wrong call – it was 50/50 – but Bevan gave it to South Africa, the home side.

At the 2007 World Cup, New Zealand played a quarterfinal against tournament hosts France in front of more than 70 000 people in Cardiff. Much to the frustration of the crowd, New Zealand dominated the possession and territory statistics, but the scoreline remained tight throughout.

The match-winning moment came at 69 minutes when, against the run of play, Frédéric Michalak broke through and offloaded to centre Yannick Jauzion, who scored.

The French crowd was ecstatic, but it was clear in the replays that the pass to Michalak in the build-up had been forward. It wasn't picked up by the touch judge or by referee Wayne Barnes, who was just 28 years old at the time. The hosts held on for the last 10 minutes and the final score was 20-18 to France. Because of a critical refereeing error, the All Blacks were knocked out. Barnes would later acknowledge that the pass had been forward.

I'm not saying referees turn a blind eye, but if there is a 50/50 call then it will almost always go to the home or more heavily fancied side. In a strange way, that call from Barnes also helped the Springboks, who avoided the All Blacks on their way to a second World Cup crown.

The World Cup that really haunts South African fans from a refereeing perspective is the 2011 edition. Having made the quarterfinals in unconvincing fashion, the Springboks had to play the Wallabies in Wellington. They were comfortably the better side and gave their performance of the tournament, but New Zealand referee Bryce Lawrence delivered an incomprehensible display of officiating and took no responsibility for anything happening around the breakdown.

It was a free-for-all, and David Pocock and the other Australian forwards benefited immensely. They were coming in from the side, playing the ball on the ground, and there was one incident in which Pocock was off his feet in the middle of the ruck and pulling the ball out with his hands. He had no right to be there, and it was one of numerous instances in which the Boks could and should have been awarded a kickable penalty.

It was such a poor refereeing display but, again, that game was played in Australasia and the Wallabies had the crowd behind them. Lawrence was not prepared to be strict on Australia and penalise them when he should have, and the 11-9 defeat meant the Springboks were knocked out of the competition as defending champions.

Even in the 2011 final between New Zealand and France in Auckland, French former players still do not understand why South African referee Craig Joubert kept telling the All Blacks to 'roll away' instead of penalising them during the closing stages. The play was taking place about 40 metres from the New Zealand line, and France would have had a relatively routine shot at goal to win the game had the penalty gone their way. France lost that final 8-7 and, again, were left wondering what might have been had a call or two been awarded to them.

After the match, Joubert said he had wanted the players, not a refereeing decision, to win the World Cup final. It is unfortunate that if the same scenario had unfolded in the first 10 minutes of the game, he probably would have penalised New Zealand just to set the tone. But because it was in New Zealand there was so much pressure on the referee from the crowd that it was very difficult for Joubert – as a human being – to penalise the All Blacks at the time, and ultimately France were the victims.

Joubert was also the referee in the 2015 quarterfinal between Australia and Scotland at Twickenham, and it was here that he ended up at the centre of one of the most controversial refereeing calls in Rugby World Cup history.

With Scotland leading 34-32, there was a moment in the dying stages of the game when the ball hit the shoulder of Scottish player, Josh Strauss, and went forward to be gathered by one of his teammates. It looked offside, and Australia was awarded the penalty which was knocked over by Bernard Foley to give the Wallabies the win.

It all happened so quickly, and Joubert did not see that the ball had ever so slightly made contact with an Australian player, Nick Phipps, after coming off Strauss. Crucially, World Rugby laws at the time meant Joubert could not ask the TMO to have another look, which was very unfair. To the naked eye, it was so difficult to spot, and the crowd was absolutely incensed.

They and the Scottish players abused Joubert to

the extent that he had to run off the field at the end of the game, looking like he was running away from his responsibility. He wasn't. He was just trying to get off the field safely and defuse what had become an ugly situation.

World Rugby came out afterwards and admitted Joubert had made a mistake. I thought this was poor because no referee would have seen that touch on the field without the help of a replay. Scotland were the 'home' side in this situation, but this was another clear example of the pressure referees have to deal with in the heated, emotional cauldron of World Cup rugby.

In Japan in 2019 there were no real major refereeing issues, apart from in South Africa's opening game against New Zealand where Rassie was not happy with how Jérôme Garcès officiated. The Springbok coach sent a number of clips to World Rugby after the game – the Boks lost 23-13 – and the refereeing body agreed with the points he made.

Importantly, Rassie went through the right channels and was rewarded later in the tournament. Garcès was appointed to handle South Africa's semifinal against Wales as well as the final against England, and he refereed both matches impeccably; none of the sides involved could have had any complaints.

I don't think it was by chance that 2019 was largely

incident-free from a refereeing perspective, when you consider that none of the sides realistically going for the title was playing at home.

Japan making the quarterfinal was an excellent effort, and one could argue that in the game against the Springboks Damian de Allende scored a perfectly legitimate try just before halftime. It wasn't awarded, though, because he was deemed to have held onto the ball on the ground and to have performed a double movement. After the match, that was shown not to be the case. Again, it was a 50/50 call that went to the home side.

Given all of this and the fact that we now have yellow and red cards coming in more regularly to prevent head injuries and promote player safety, there is a massive emphasis on playing within the laws when coaching a team.

Coaches must make absolutely certain their players understand the way referees are implementing the laws, because in the past there has been a noticeable difference in interpretation between officials from the northern and southern hemispheres. While those differences are still apparent, consistency in applying the law has improved significantly.

But if we accept that teams who are heavily fancied by the crowds will be favoured by the referees – as Ireland

and France will be in 2023 – then that is something to prepare for. No northern hemisphere side has won a World Cup since 2003, and there will be a feeling that 2023 is their turn.

Faced with that kind of momentum, it can become very difficult for a team to compete against one of the favourites in a quarterfinal or semifinal. You might find that the 50/50 calls we have seen throughout the tournament's history start going against you, so what can you do to get a fair crack of the whip? Bear in mind that the Springboks couldn't do it on their northern hemisphere tour in 2022, when they were on the wrong side of some crucial decisions in their losses to Ireland and France.

South Africa will have to ensure they go into this World Cup squeaky clean. They need to be within the laws in absolutely every department. They have to scrum within the laws, they need to ensure their driving maul is within the laws, and their physicality – such a huge weapon for them – must not cross over into penalisable territory.

The way they carry the ball, clean rucks and challenge on the ground has to be so precise that they do not give the referees the chance to blow them up. It could require just one head clash that's a touch too high or one forearm leading into the face of a defender for the Springboks to lose a player to a card, and it is very difficult to win a big knockout game with 14 men on the field.

It looks like organisers might adopt an 'orange card' at the 2023 World Cup, which would allow referees to show a player a yellow card that can be upgraded to red once he has left the field and the TMO has studied the footage. The idea is to speed up play by not having to sit through numerous replays before a referee takes a final decision.

While I agree with the initiative, I still think we are going to see a lot of cards at the tournament because of how strict the safety laws are. So many mitigating circumstances have been ignored by referees in recent years because they have been so worried about being accused of not taking the concussion protocols seriously, and they would rather err on the side of safety.

I have no doubt that a card, or cards, will influence one of the major games in France – maybe a playoff – and leave one side feeling bitterly unlucky. No side will go onto the field intending to break the law, but the margins are so fine these days that I think it will inevitably happen. It is so easy to misjudge a tackle and get it even slightly wrong, which could have dire consequences.

I hope that this year, in the Rugby Championship and in their warm-ups before the World Cup, the Springboks conduct all communication about refereeing through the right channels and protocols. I hope there will not be any use of social media to humiliate the referees, because as I observed earlier on, that does far more harm than good in terms of how referees treat the Boks.

As it turns out, Nigel Owens did not accept an offer from SA Rugby to be its refereeing consultant for the World Cup, and while that was disappointing, thinking along those lines is definitely the way to go.

And I do think Jacques Nienaber has a calmer, more dispassionate, more objective view than Rassie sometimes does after a game. He doesn't appear to get as emotionally involved, and it is very hard to criticise the comments he makes in interviews, even if the Boks have been refereed unfairly.

Jacques has always been very mature in that space and I think that stands the Springboks in good stead heading into the World Cup. He always encourages his players to get better and learn from their mistakes, and he never uses the referee as an excuse for a poor result. The longer you take that position, the more secure referees feel when they are assigned to your matches.

That is exactly what the Springboks need after a difficult period in which their relationship with referees has been severely tested since the 2021 British & Irish Lions tour. If a referee is not operating under the fear of being lambasted on social media, he may be more inclined to give the Springboks a 50/50 call. That is just how the psychology of these things works.

Rugby is a game in which the referee can penalise one team 16 times and the other team six times, and be completely correct in all his decisions. What you must ask, though, is if the referee is looking at both sides equally. If a referee is looking at one side more than the other, for whatever reason, that will translate into more penalties being awarded.

Given their recent history, I believe South Africa will need to be mindful of exactly that heading into the World Cup, where high-profile fixtures against Ireland and Scotland await in the pool stages.

You must understand the referee, the way he goes about his business and what he watches out for. If your scrutiny shows, for example, that a referee favours a side that runs with the ball and you play a game that is based on kicking and defence, there needs to be an acceptance that you will be penalised more.

All aspects of a referee's performance have to be analysed, and I have no doubt that Rassie and Jacques will be more prepared than anyone given the intricacy of the detail they studied in 2019.

Still, from a South African perspective this is going to be a very difficult World Cup to win. The Springboks are in a tricky pool and their recent history of criticising referees makes their task even tougher. But there has been a period of peace since Rassie's sanction, and the relationship needs to continue along amicable lines in all refereeing communication with World Rugby, both before and during the 2023 World Cup.

The Springboks must be a team that look as though they are complying with and accepting World Rugby's protocols. If they don't, and if they rail against perceived injustice or unfairness, then I don't see it ending well for them.

I do think South Africa's move to northern hemisphere competitions, where they have been exposed to a range of referees in the URC and European Champions and Challenge cups, works in their favour.

Coaches from the Stormers, Sharks, Bulls and Lions have had opportunities for regular communication with the URC refereeing committee, which is headed by former South African referee Tappe Henning. He is someone who is receptive to the South African coaches, and he has acknowledged that there have been frustrations.

There have been issues about the quality of the refereeing in the URC and with how the game is being played. South Africans like to get messy at the breakdown, for example, whereas up north, referees do not like players interfering there.

I am sure Rassie will be in communication with the franchise coaches to gain insight into how refereeing in the URC has worked, and I think the players themselves will have benefited from their regular exposure to both

South African and northern hemisphere referees.

They are now familiar with several of the guys who will be refereeing at the World Cup, such as Wayne Barnes, Luke Pearce and Mathieu Raynal, and there is a good chance those men will referee South Africa at some point, especially in their pool fixtures against Ireland and Scotland.

While the South African players have come to know these referees better, that is not the case over in New Zealand and Australia, where the All Blacks and Wallabies have been playing Super Rugby Pacific.

The URC teams have also been playing under the same laws that will be applied at the World Cup, while New Zealand and Australia have tweaked things slightly. They are playing a fast-paced game that encourages ball-in-hand attack where the No. 8 and No. 9 are never under pressure from the base of a scrum, and everything is in favour of the side with the ball.

When they get to the World Cup and sides attack them at the set piece, I wonder how much New Zealand, in particular, will be able to adapt after playing in a competition that doesn't promote double-shoving scrums and set piece dominance.

I cannot emphasise enough the importance of the referee's role in contributing to teams getting through games, particularly when they are evenly matched – something that is very much the case between South Africa, France, New Zealand and Ireland. All fixtures between these sides are going to be extremely close and tough to call.

The team that is playing with the strongest set of fans behind them, or who go in with the momentum of being popular, even being the favourites, will absolutely hold the advantage. It is just one more hurdle the Springboks will have to overcome if they are to defend their title successfully.

8
Packs and halfbacks
... where it's won

There isn't a pundit around who doesn't believe the 2023 Rugby World Cup, more than any other in the tournament's history, is wide open and could go so many ways.

Even though the draw for the pool stages and quarterfinals is one-sided, this is still a very difficult tournament to predict. On their day, any of France, Ireland, South Africa, New Zealand and Scotland – all in the same half of the draw and on a collision course for the quarterfinals – could beat each other.

Those matches could be decided by a single moment of brilliance or a refereeing call, but going a bit deeper than that I think the history of the World Cup gives us some clues as to who is more likely to be successful.

For me, there are two areas in which World Cups are won: the pack and the halfbacks. Every side will have their stars who are capable of changing games by themselves, but as a general rule, the sides that have done well at World Cups are those with the most consistently impactful forwards, and a halfback pair expertly and accurately controlling things behind them.

Even as far back as 1995, the Springboks had a pack that included really gifted players such as Os du Randt and Mark Andrews, while Joost van der Westhuizen and Joel Stransky were pivotal at scrum half and fly half respectively.

The Boks weren't the favourites, but they had a powerful pack of forwards who provided them with the base to achieve something special. They had a huge amount of passion, and defensively they were able to hold sides out all the way through the competition, including New Zealand in the final.

I thought Joost and Joel were both brilliant at that tournament. There was always absolute clarity about who was going to play No. 9 and No. 10, and ultimately it was Joel's drop goal that got the Springboks over the line.

In 1999 you had George Gregan and Stephen Larkham together, and that is still considered the greatest halfback pairing in the history of Australian rugby, maybe even the history of the game. Larkham's drop goal in the semifinal against the South African team I was coaching is often spoken about as the moment that won the Wallabies the World Cup that year, but he and Gregan had played so many games together and had been instrumental in their side's success long before that moment.

Of course, that was the last time Australia won the Webb Ellis Cup, and I don't think it is a coincidence that it happened with those two exceptional players in the side. The Wallabies also had an outstanding line-out that year under John Eales, and while they didn't have the most dominant scrum, they were able to play a continuity game because of their dependability at line-out time. Then they had Owen Finegan, whose ball-carrying was brilliant.

What happened in 2003 further strengthens my case. There was Jonny Wilkinson's famous right-footed drop goal in the final that sunk the Wallabies, and alongside scrum half Matt Dawson he was playing behind the best pack in the world. England had Steve Thompson at hooker, Jason Leonard in the front row, Martin Johnson and Ben Kay at lock, Richard Hill and Neil Back at flank and Lawrence Dallaglio at No. 8. Most of those names would have been strong World XV candidates in 2003. They were all very impressive.

In 2007, the Springboks had Fourie du Preez at scrum half – also the best in the world in his position that year – with the dependable Butch James outside of him. Butch wasn't the goalkicker – that responsibility belonged to the eagle-eyed Percy Montgomery – but in the game plan the Boks had, he was incredibly strong as a defensive fly half and brilliant with his territorial kicking.

They played behind an immensely powerful pack that included some of the greats of South African rugby: Os du Randt, Bakkies Botha, Victor Matfield, Schalk Burger, John Smit ... they were all in the form of their lives, and some of the best in the world at the time.

The 2011 World Cup was a bit of an anomaly because the All Blacks went into the final with their fourth-choice fly half, but in 2015 they were able to field Aaron Smith and the great Dan Carter as their halfback combination.

People often forget Carter's drop goal in the semifinal against South Africa that year when they were down to 14 men after Jerome Kaino had received a yellow card. In the time Kaino was off the field the All Blacks scored three points and the Springboks none, and Carter showed a real maturity in how he controlled that period of the game.

Again, that was the best halfback pairing in the world that year, playing behind another outstanding pack that included Kieran Read, Brodie Retallick and Richie McCaw.

We saw the same trend in 2019, when Faf de Klerk and Handré Pollard combined in the most effective fashion, even if it didn't always make the most entertaining viewing. Pollard's kicking display against Wales in the semifinal was world-class, and crucial in securing a place in the final. The Springboks also had comfortably the best pack in the tournament. They were a massive scrummaging unit with a 6/2 forwards/backs bench – the 'Bomb Squad' – who were as good as the starters and helped the Springboks win numerous penalties.

In every World Cup there has been a key forward who I thought was instrumental in helping their side to glory. I've never been a great fan of singling out individuals because I believe every success comes as a result of the collective effort, but these are the guys I thought were particularly exceptional at each showpiece over the years:

1995: Os du Randt. Outstanding. The spine of the Boks.

1999: Owen Finegan. Brilliant ball-carrying for the Wallabies.

2003: Richard Hill. The unsung hero of the England side in the semifinals and final.

2007: Victor Matfield. His mastery of the line-outs gave the Springboks a real edge.

2011: Tony Woodcock. The best loose head prop in the world at the time.

2015: Jerome Kaino. Such a gifted player, and brilliant throughout that World Cup.

2019: Pieter-Steph du Toit. 'Player of the Year' and a magnificent specimen of a rugby player.

When we consider all of that history, then look ahead to the 2023 World Cup in France, we should be examining how the title contenders stack up in terms of their halfbacks and their packs. As an exercise, I have given each of the contenders a rating out of 10 in both categories.

We'll start with the packs, where I have also included an individual for each of the 'big four' sides who I believe will be hugely important to their cause in 2023. Let's see how they stack up.

South Africa

The Springboks will enter the 2023 World Cup with largely the same personnel, as we have mentioned, which means they will once more have an outstanding starting pack and an equally capable 'Bomb Squad'. They have probably the best tight five in the world. They will be strong in the scrum, line-out and driving maul. The Boks have so much depth in this department that it doesn't matter who they field. They are blessed with quality from No. 1 to No. 8.

Key player: Eben Etzebeth

I thought Etzebeth should have been named World Rugby Player of the Year in 2022, and I think he could potentially have a massive World Cup. He has already secured his status as a Springbok great but the 31-year-old enforcer is still at the peak of his career and is considered by many to be the most powerful second-rower in the game.

Pack rating: 9/10

France

The French have adopted South Africa's World Cup-winning recipe by picking a huge pack of forwards, and they also have a very good bench full of impact players who come on with intensity, purpose and an ability to provide an injection of power. They now understand how crucial it is to have a dominant pack. Their scrums and line-outs function superbly, and it is very difficult to separate them from the Boks.

Key player: Grégory Alldritt

The French No. 8 is an exceptional rugby player, and when we talk about the hosts having a dominant pack, he is at the heart of it. He carries and tackles strongly, slows down and steals ball, and is a force in all departments. He showed exactly that in the 2023 Champions Cup final, guiding La Rochelle to a superb 27-26 win over Leinster to bag their second successive European title.

Pack rating: 9/10

Ireland

Ireland have a solid pack of forwards but not a dominant scrum. They are brilliant at the line-out and in phase play, and it is particularly in those areas that they set up their attacking platform. Make no mistake, their scrum is still very capable and they will have joy there against most opposition. But against the likes of South Africa and France, it is an area where they could find themselves under pressure.

Key player: James Ryan

Standing at 2.03 metres, this lock forward has developed so well and has become a mainstay of the Irish pack. He has captained Ireland, too, when Johnny Sexton has been unavailable, and his all-round game – from stealing line-outs to ball-carrying and defence – has made him a crucial cog in the Irish machine.

Pack rating: 8/10

New Zealand

Jason Ryan joining the All Blacks as forwards coach has come just in time. This was an area of huge concern for them not long ago, but Ryan has got them playing far more directly and using their tight five. They are vastly improved heading into the World Cup. I would have given them 5/10 before Ryan came on board but I think they are a lot better than that now.

Key player: Ardie Savea

It seems as if Savea never has a bad game for New Zealand. He has the attributes of strength and physicality

125

that the All Blacks crave in their pack, but also the skill and pace to be the link between forwards and backs that allows New Zealand to be the attacking force they are.

Pack rating: 7/10

Now let's turn our attention to the all-important halfbacks.

South Africa

I think we can expect to see continuity here with Pollard and De Klerk starting, even if there are now other options in both positions. There will be no lack of experience or big-match temperament there. They have played together for a sustained period, and intimately understand each other and the Springbok game plan. What you see is what you get with these two, and they do it so accurately.

Halfbacks rating: 8/10

France

Antoine Dupont and Romain Ntamack are a lethal combination. Ntamack is not the goalkicker – they have fullback Thomas Ramos for that job – but this pairing is a major weapon for France. Dupont is widely regarded as the best scrum half and one of the most naturally gifted players in the world, while Ntamack has shown a brilliant ability to pull the strings by understanding when to kick, pass or try something different. He is a wonderful tactical kicker and distributor. France, like the Boks, have tremendous continuity in these positions.

Halfbacks rating: 9/10

Ireland

Scrum half Jamison Gibson-Park and veteran playmaker Johnny Sexton have come together over the last year or so, and they have proven to be superb. The way Ireland play is aided by Gibson-Park's speed in getting to the breakdown and his ability to make good decisions about whether to go open side or blind side. He brings in his runners expertly, playing up his forwards through that box attack they have. He's head and shoulders above of any other scrum half in Ireland in the way he does that. He isn't a danger man on the break, but his tactical kicking is good and his continuity play is sound. Similarly, Sexton is a step ahead of any other fly half in Ireland in terms of his understanding of the team's plan, his competitiveness and how he drives the game.

Halfbacks rating: 9/10

New Zealand

The All Blacks are likely to field Aaron Smith and Richie Mo'unga, and they will have good continuity and experience there if that is how they set up. They are both extremely dangerous players, but I still feel that a lot of New Zealand's success will be determined by their pack of forwards. There was a period in which the All Blacks were chopping and changing between Mo'unga and Beauden Barrett, who is obviously a hugely exciting option, but I think they have finally settled on Mo'unga as their kicker and fly half.

Halfbacks rating: 7/10

These, for me, are the areas where the World Cup will be won or lost. Of course there are other sides who will be backing themselves for the title, but I feel these are the four to beat. But let's look at some of the other teams and where they are in these departments.

Scotland

Ben White and Finn Russell are likely to be the Scottish halfbacks. Having tried different combinations, it seems as though coach Gregor Townsend has settled on Russell. The issue here for me is the continuity factor. White is a relatively recent addition, so while this combination might be the most logical fit for the World Cup after a few experiments, it doesn't come with years of being tried and tested.

In terms of the pack, I think the improvement here is the reason Scotland climbed to No. 5 in the world in 2022. Outside of our 'big four', Scotland probably have the best balance, and much of that is down to a pack that has bulked up and strengthened at the set piece. They can no longer be viewed as a pushover by any side.

Pack rating: 7/10

Halfback rating: 7/10

England

When we look at teams through the lens of consistency and continuity, England's problems become clear. They are looking at Jack van Poortvliet at scrum half and either Owen Farrell or Marcus Smith at fly half. They still have to make their choice, and not having an answer to that question this close to a World Cup is a problem.

Their pack, though, is where the real issue lies. I don't think there are any players there who would command a place in the French or South African starting lineups, for example, and it will be very difficult for them to take on sides of that quality and push them to the wire.

Pack rating: 5/10

Halfback rating: 6/10

Australia

Again, it doesn't look like the Wallabies have settled on anything. You have Nic White, Quade Cooper, Bernard Foley and a new coach in Eddie Jones who, despite being an Australian rugby mastermind, has not had the time in charge to find any finality and certainty on the best combination.

Like England, the Wallabies have not shown any dominance in their pack. It's all a bit lightweight for me, and they lack the firepower and muscle that the top sides all have in abundance.

Pack rating: 5/10
Halfback rating: 6/10

Argentina

The Pumas are slightly better positioned than the other sides in their half of the draw, but they also haven't really settled on a fly half. They have Gonzalo Bertranou at scrum half, but at No. 10 it's either Nicolás Sánchez or Tomás Albornoz, who played when Sánchez was injured. But I do think they've had more continuity there than other sides, and all three players I've mentioned are quality players.

As has often been the case, Argentina's pack remains a strength for them. It has become a bit of a rugby stereotype that Argentina will always be a force when it comes to scrummaging, and while they are nowhere near the level of the Springboks or France, that still holds true. They have the physicality to impose themselves on their opposition.

Pack rating: 7/10
Halfback rating: 7/10

Wales

The Welsh have real issues. They have Rhys Webb as their starting scrum half with Tomos Williams coming off the bench, while Dan Biggar will surely be the man Warren Gatland – back in charge – opts for as his fly half. Owen Williams has played there but Gatland has always been a fan of Biggar. When the side are not doing well there is often chopping and changing at No. 9 and No. 10, and that doesn't help in the context of a World Cup.

The Wales pack is nothing to write home about, and a lack of impetus there has been a huge factor in their struggles during the build-up to France.

Pack rating: 5/10
Halfback rating: 5/10

Good packs and halfbacks win you World Cups. It's that simple for me, because that is what history has shown us. It's why I believe South Africa, France and Ireland are the favourites to lift the trophy in 2023, while New Zealand are probably also in the mix having turned the corner with their forwards.

Of course there will still be moments of individual brilliance and X factor that could change matches, and it always helps to have players who can do something special. The teams that produce those moments of magic, however, are generally those with strong packs and clever halfbacks who can spot the opportunity when a certain play might be on.

It's about identifying the moment – it might be a penalty advantage or a turnover – and knowing when there is a window to try something different. It is the halfbacks who generally drive those decisions, but from loose and open play, sometimes it comes down to instinct.

In that area, the Springboks are incredibly gifted. With the likes of Cheslin Kolbe, Lukhanyo Am and, more recently, Kurt-Lee Arendse in the mix, they possess that ability to produce something special out of nothing. And while that will not be the formula for victory at France 2023, it is such a luxury to have.

It all starts from having laid a solid foundation up front, though, and not all teams can do that. If you look at a side such as Fiji, for example, almost every player in the team is special. They have locks who can run like wings, wings who can hand-off like locks, and individually their players are all capable of extraordinary things.

They are drowning in skills and are always a joy to watch, but their inability to match the tight five of the major nations and the pressure they face at scrum and maul time are their downfall. I do believe there is a place for extraordinary individual talent, but usually it comes in teams with good structure.

When Makazole Mapimpi and Lukhanyo Am combined for the Springboks' first try in the 2019 World Cup final, they did so in spectacular fashion. Am's no-look pass to his left was a moment rich in individual skill, and it will go down as one of the great moments in South African rugby history. But even that famous try was the result of defensive pressure in the pack that forced the turnover in the first place.

It wasn't as if the try came through the Springboks throwing the ball around with the aim of entertaining the crowd. It came because of sustained pressure – through set piece, defence and accurate tactical kicking – that eventually broke the English and created that small window of opportunity.

When coaches pick their squads and starting lineups, individual skill doesn't play as big a role as some might think. The player must fit into what the side is looking to achieve. You can't depend on any one player to win a game. France, for example, cannot depend on Dupont alone, even though he is the current World Rugby

Player of the Year and an exceptional talent.

If a whole game plan revolves around one player, then it makes it much easier for an opposing team to come up with a counter. None of the top sides in the world is doing that, and they all have their own unique, deliberate models for success.

The one thing these blueprints all have in common, though, is that they are based on the pack providing the platform for the halfbacks to control the game. In that space the top four sides are so evenly matched, and it promises to make for edge-of-your-seat viewing.

9
Leadership and trust
... coaching and captaincy

No Rugby World Cup has ever been won without complete trust existing between the head coach and his captain, and between the captain and his team. Any coach will tell you that. Trust is crucial.

Over the years, in my own coaching career, I began to understand this more and more, and at times I had to learn it the hard way.

The reason I'm so painfully aware of the importance of complete trust and faith in a leadership group is because I saw first-hand what happened when we went to the 1999 World Cup and I lost the trust of the team. I saw how hard it was to get that team to perform.

Before the tournament, hosted by Wales and also

played in England, Scotland, Ireland and France, I made a naive error in dropping Gary Teichmann – the best leader in our group – because of form. It caused major issues.

I offered Rassie Erasmus the captaincy, and thought he was going to take it and that I could work well with him. But he turned me down for a number of reasons. One was that he supported Gary and wanted him to be at the World Cup. Rassie felt that if he accepted the captaincy it would look as if he had been waiting to take over from Gary, and he didn't want to give that impression.

I then offered it to Joost van der Westhuizen, who accepted it, but I don't think it ended up being the right move. Joost was a very self-driven individual, but to be a great captain you have to continuously think about other people and not only your own performance or success. He and I did not have a solid, trusting relationship with each other. It was just like that.

Joost was very strongly Afrikaans and he saw me as profoundly English, and he also didn't agree with the call I had made on Teichmann. I couldn't reach the same closeness and understanding with Joost that I had with Gary. We just didn't have that connection.

We did everything we could to try to win that World Cup, but I strongly believe that we lost the semifinal to Australia as much because of the leadership trust deficiency between Joost and me as because of Stephen Larkham's drop goal.

I've often looked back and wondered: if we had had Gary on the field as captain when we went three points up in the second half of extra time, would we have had the leadership to calm everyone down and give us the composure to get over the line? Unfortunately I had already made the error, so it wasn't to be.

I still believe that was the biggest mistake of my coaching career.

The team I had through 1997 and 1998 went on a run of winning 17 out of 18 Test matches. But in 1999, after a couple of key injuries, they didn't perform quite as well. That influenced my decision to drop Gary, and from that moment on there was a trust issue between me and the team from which we couldn't recover.

If I could drop the captain, I could drop any one of the players, and that affected them negatively. There was an immediate withdrawal of the connection that I believe is so important between a coach and his team.

I tried never to do that again in the other coaching jobs I had at Stade Français and Italy. The lesson I learned in 1999 is one that I kept with me throughout the rest of my coaching career and it's a moment I wish I could have back.

For me, there are a few key pillars – they all begin with a 'C', so they are easy to remember – to building trust in a rugby team environment. In a perfect situation, the head coach will trust and be trusted by his captain, and that will filter down to the rest of the team.

Competence

Trust is built on competence. The coach must know his subject matter inside out so that any player who goes to him with a question or a suggestion will be given an authoritative answer backed up by facts and figures.

It could be a question about why a side is playing a certain way, and if the reasoning behind the answer is sound it will help to build trust in the coach's thinking behind the plan.

The captain, too, needs to show his competence in the way he plays – he should be picked on ability in his position, first – and in how he understands the tactics of the side and the game as a whole.

Essentially, the coach and captain need to know what they are doing, and there can be no doubts about that in the playing group.

Communication

For both captain and coach, proper communication is essential. Clear, concise and respectful communication from coach to captain must be carried down to the players.

It needs to be completely aligned from top to bottom

with accurate messaging that the team understands and believes in.

Think about it tin terms of education: a teacher must not only communicate the facts that he or she knows but ensure that students in the class absorb that same knowledge. The way important information is communicated can be vital in determining success or failure.

Connection

Here, I'm not just talking about the connection between a head coach and his captain on a rugby level. It needs to go much deeper than that. The connection has to be on a personal level, too; the coach and captain should know each other as people. They must respect and admire each other's personality traits and find out as much as they possibly can about each other.

Knowing somebody's background and where they come from helps in understanding them more fully, and if coaches and captains make that investment in each other and their players, the reward is trust.

It can be something as simple as the way they say 'Good morning' when walking through a room. Are they being sincere in that greeting or are they just saying it because they have to?

The best leaders all make time for those around them, taking a genuine interest. How was your weekend? How are your kids doing at school? Engaging with players on that level is incredibly important for coaches and captains in forming a connection. Ultimately, it makes it so much easier for the players to buy into the vision and produce the goods on the field.

Commitment

The commitment of the head coach and captain to the team needs to be evident. It can never be in any doubt. If we go back and again use the example of Rassie's infamous refereeing video aimed at World Rugby, I don't think I have ever seen any more commitment than that. Rassie was prepared to be punished to give his team the best opportunity to win the British & Irish Lions series, and he was completely committed to the cause.

For captains, showing commitment comes in how they train. Are they prepared to put in the extra yards on the training field and in the gym to try to secure the best possible result at the weekend? In all things leaders do – on and off the field – commitment to the end goal must always be visible.

Consistency

There needs to be consistency in the way a captain and coach behave, and in the way a coach selects. There needs to be consistency in behaviour, so the players know what they are going to get and are never surprised or shocked by an outburst or a sudden change in emotion.

Whether you win or lose, there must be consistency in your thought process, and that will help build trust. A captain can't start screaming and shouting at his players when he is having a bad day. The way he transfers information needs to be dependable.

Confidence

Once a leadership group starts to display these attributes, a confidence develops that can be extremely powerful. It is confidence in what the head coach is saying, confidence in the captain to operate as the leader of the pack, and ultimately the confidence that the players have in each other, their ability, and their shared vision.

If players have confidence, it allows them to go about their business with freedom, safe in the knowledge that they are on the right track and prepared as well as they can be.

If all of these 'Cs' are nurtured by the leadership team of the coach and captain, then trust is the end result – and that is really what you need. Trust in each other. Trust in the process. It is impossible to overstate how important that is. Without that trust, you can still progress in the Rugby World Cup, but you will lose critical games. I know this better than anyone.

Since South Africa first played in the Rugby World Cup, all winning sides have had trust between the coach and his captain, and the captain and his team.

1995: Kitch Christie and Francois Pienaar.
1999: Rod Macqueen and John Eales.
2003: Clive Woodward and Martin Johnson.
2007: Jake White and John Smit.
2011: Graham Henry and Richie McCaw.
2015: Steve Hansen and Richie McCaw.
2019: Rassie Erasmus and Siya Kolisi.

In each of these cases, had the victorious side not ended up winning the World Cup it certainly wouldn't have been down to a trust issue between coach and captain.

I'm not saying there haven't been other combinations where trust was obvious, but I am saying that where there isn't that trust, it is incredibly difficult to win this competition. No team has won the World Cup where there has been a dysfunctional relationship between the coach, his captain and the team.

Apart from my error in dropping Gary Teichmann, there are other sides who have learnt this lesson the hard way.

At the 2007 World Cup in France, England had highly publicised issues with their head coach, Brian Ashton. They made the final, where they lost to the

Springboks, and the team ultimately decided not to play the style of rugby Ashton had coached.

They went back to a more conservative style and decided to coach themselves in those last couple of games, according to Lawrence Dallaglio. They were outplayed in their 15-6 loss to the Boks in the tournament decider. When a coach's charges mutiny, it just doesn't work.

In 2011 there was another example when France had major issues with their head coach, Marc Lièvremont, and there was a player revolt against him mid-tournament. It was very typically French when things are not going well, but the team still got through their semifinal against Wales – they won 9-8 after a first-half red card to Sam Warburton – and into the final against the All Blacks.

They lost that game 8-7, and it was a remarkable run deep into the competition when one considers the issues there were between players and coach.

If we jump to 2015, when England were playing at home, there had been a loss of confidence in Stuart Lancaster as head coach. England didn't didn't even manage to get out of their pool after defeats to Wales and Australia.

In 2019, meanwhile, I strongly believe that New Zealand had no clarity around selection. They didn't have a proper blind side flank, they didn't know who their fly half was, they didn't have a ball-carrying No. 12 and they had no certainty at fullback. They went into the semifinal against England believing their style of rugby was going to be good enough, but they got hammered. It wasn't that they had lost confidence in Steve Hansen, but there was no clarity and consistency in selection.

There are examples of teams that reached the business end of a World Cup and had a good chance of winning, but because of slight trust issues around a lack of consistency, communication, confidence or clarity, they fell just short. We were one of those teams, and I believe we could have made the final in 1999 – and won it – had we got those things right.

Let's apply this line of thinking to 2023 and see where the teams are. I'll give them scores out of 10 again, this time considering coaches and captains, and how they fit together as a leadership pairing.

Ireland

Ireland have great consistency. Coach Andy Farrell has been there for three or four years, and captain Johnny Sexton has worked under him throughout that tenure. Sexton, of course, was in deep trouble with World Rugby following his tirade at South African referee Jaco Peyper following the 2023 Champions Cup final between Leinster and La Rochelle that created the possibility of a ban. In spite of this, Farrell and Sexton still have a strong bond and they are clearly aligned in Ireland's World Cup build-up; there is a belief that starts at the top and filters down to the playing squad.

Ireland are very focused going into this World Cup, having won a Six Nations and a series away to New Zealand, and an overwhelming sense of confidence has come from those performances and results. I think they are as strong as they've ever been in terms of trust in their leadership.

Leadership rating: 9/10

France

It is exactly the same for the 2023 hosts, who have flourished under the clear, consistent and thoughtful coaching of Fabien Galthié. As captain he has Antoine Dupont, who has commanded the respect of his peers through his obvious status as one of the best players in the world.

Since he arrived in 2019, Galthié has shown consistency in selection and playing style and he has assembled a team of very capable coaches around him. There is real belief in a French team that at one stage in the build-up to the World Cup won 14 straight Test matches.

They won the 2022 Six Nations, and from top to bottom there is complete trust in the vision and efforts aimed at winning a maiden World Cup in front of a home crowd in Paris on 28 October.

Leadership rating: 9/10

South Africa

There is absolute trust and consistency between head coach Jacques Nienaber and director of rugby Rassie Erasmus, who combine in a rather unique way to form the Springbok coaching leadership. They have worked together all their lives, and after what they achieved in 2019 there is massive belief in their ability to win another World Cup.

They have also always had a great relationship with Siya Kolisi, who has grown into a fine captain in every respect. Siya has the respect of his coaches and his teammates, but the obvious worry is the fact that he is injured. At the time I wrote this book there was no clarity on whether Siya would make the World Cup, and that is a serious disruption to a leadership group planning its title defence.

There are options beyond Kolisi if he is ruled out – Handré Pollard, Lukhanyo Am and Eben Etzebeth all have the experience and respect of their teammates – but it is impossible to overlook everything Kolisi has achieved during his Springbok captaincy. He has built total trust between the players and the coaches and his overall contribution has been immense, so this development has to be seen as a setback to the leadership group. That is the only reason I am scoring the Springboks slightly lower than France and Ireland.

Leadership rating: 8/10

New Zealand

New Zealand have a coach, Ian Foster, who has been heavily criticised and had to hang onto his job for dear life in 2022. There has been a lot of media pressure about the All Blacks' performances heading into the World Cup, which have included a Test defeat to Argentina and a series loss to Ireland at home for the first time.

Foster was kept on but made significant changes to his backroom staff, which hasn't been good for continuity and consistency. There remains a bit of noise about the coaching setup.

Foster has a captain in Sam Cane who has often been missing due to concussion or other injury, and it seems he constantly needs to justify his place in the team with performances.

The All Blacks certainly aren't as calm and stable in the leadership department as they would have liked heading into France 2023. Foster is a very good coach and Cane is an accomplished captain, but I don't believe the preparation has instilled complete trust in the progress the All Blacks have made before they go to France aiming for a fourth Webb Ellis Cup.

Leadership rating: 7/10

Scotland

Scotland have Gregor Townsend, one of the all-time legends of their game, as their head coach, and I think he is largely trustworthy. Their captain, Jamie Ritchie, also seems like a very decent guy. I don't know him well and he has had only a year or so of captaining, but by all accounts he is a figure who has the respect of the dressing room.

The big potential issue Scotland have involves play-maker Finn Russell. Townsend has had personal issues with Russell in the past, and the player's personal discipline problems have seen him dropped. Russell is not captain, of course, but he is a strong team leader, and as fly half he is the driver of their philosophy on the field.

I wouldn't go as far as saying Russell is a trouble-maker, but he has proved difficult to control at times. He can be red-hot when he is on form, but it will be a concern that he also has the tendency to drop his head when his side needs him most.

Leadership rating: 7/10

England

There has been significant disruption to England's World Cup plans with the sudden sacking of Eddie Jones as head coach in 2022. That was a massive call, as Jones was the orchestrator of their 2019 World Cup journey to the final.

The Rugby Football Union has opted for Steve Borthwick, and while he is hugely respected as a former England captain and title-winning coach with Leicester Tigers, it all feels a bit rushed.

Owen Farrell is Borthwick's captain, and there are concerns there. Farrell can be hot-headed in how he questions referees. He is incredibly competitive, and while you never want to take that away, he has to remain calm and measured when communicating with the officials. I have a feeling that when he is under pressure, Farrell gets a bit emotional, and I think that could work against England.

Leadership rating: 6/10

Australia

Like England, the Wallabies took the plunge of making a very late coaching change, replacing Dave Rennie with Jones. I felt that was harsh on Rennie, but the sudden availability of Jones after he lost the England job was too attractive for Rugby Australia to turn down. Jones is an interesting human being who has usually had very good short-term and World Cup success with his sides.

It's difficult to gauge trust levels when talking about Jones because he is a hard taskmaster and never seems to keep assistant coaches for too long. He clearly finds his coaching staff expendable, so I wouldn't associate trust with Jones. I view him as a hard worker, a massive disciplinarian and a guy who tells everyone exactly where they stand. He is prepared to drop a player in an instant if he is not performing.

The captaincy issue in Australia is also complex.

Michael Hooper had previously walked away from the job because of personal issues, but he has now been confirmed as a co-captain alongside veteran prop James Slipper. It is the first time the Wallabies have appointed co-captains for a World Cup, and it will be very interesting to see how that untested dynamic unfolds.

Leadership rating: 6/10

Argentina

The more I look at things, the more I start liking Argentina's chances. They are on the easier side of the draw and I believe they have what it takes to reach the semifinals.

In Australian head coach Michael Cheika the Pumas have put their faith in a highly volatile individual, but he is so clearly committed to the cause of his team that I think he has earned their trust. Cheika is charismatic, passionate, hugely competitive and prepared to do whatever it takes to secure victory. In many ways, he is not dissimilar to Rassie Erasmus. He just wants the best for his team.

Their captain, Julián Montoya, is closing in on 100 Test caps and since 2021 has been playing at the highest level with Leicester Tigers in the English Premiership. He is a superb leader, always so calm and unflappable under pressure, and he has the trust of his teammates.

Leadership rating: 7/10

Wales

Warren Gatland – back in charge of Wales, to try to salvage their World Cup – can certainly be trusted, because he's been there and done it before. The one thing that strikes me, though, is that he has had Shaun Edwards with him as his defence specialist wherever he has coached and they have worked very well together. Edwards is now with France and no longer available to Gatland, and I think that will have an impact.

To make the challenge even greater, Welsh rugby is experiencing all sorts of difficulties, from players threatening to strike to none of its franchises making the top eight in the URC.

There are also question marks hovering over Gatland's World Cup selection and whether he will pick an experienced, older team or a younger, talented team without the experience. There is so much uncertainty accompanying Welsh rugby right now, even though they have their seasoned coach back.

Ken Owens, the Wales captain, is a vastly experienced hooker and is widely respected by his peers. He is well into his thirties now and has a good understanding of how to approach referees. He also has experience under Gatland.

Alun Wyn Jones was Gatland's previous Wales captain, but in Owens he has an extremely able replacement. He is not only an excellent hooker but is understated and respected by referees. His relationship with Gatland will be a close one, I would think.

Leadership rating: 6/10

For me, Ireland and France enter this World Cup with the strongest leadership groups and coaching setups. They have good trust throughout their systems, and captains who have been around for a while.

The same can be said of the Springboks, but the issue for them is whether the injury to their captain affects his ability to start. If Siya Kolisi is there and he can play to his full ability, the Springboks would be a 9/10 for me. But if there is a new captain on a stage as big as the World Cup, that will be an unwanted development.

I feel that Kolisi's contribution to the Springboks since 2018 is so immense that it's impossible to measure. He has grown in his leadership in every way possible and is such an inspiration, both to the players with whom he shares the field and to the South Africans he represents at home and in the stands.

Just by being on the field, Kolisi lifts everybody around him, and he has all the attributes that make a fantastic captain. So much of that is about being calm under pressure and in the way captains communicate with the referees; and if you look at World Cup-winning captains since 1995, they all had that. Your captain has to control his own team and the referee.

John Smit was superb at it in 2007, speaking to referees with so much respect that they responded by viewing him and the Springboks favourably. Siya, too, has been critical in this department. He is such a humble guy who is willing to share leadership responsibilities, but he has become stronger as a leader in how he presents his team's position to referees.

The way he handled the British & Irish Lions series in 2021 illustrates that perfectly. The confidence he gained from the World Cup triumph in 2019, I believe, helped him take his leadership to new heights, and his worth and influence were seen against the Lions when the Boks needed to stay calm in a situation that was drowning in tension and emotion.

The team that wins the 2023 World Cup will have a captain that handles the referee expertly, giving his team the best opportunity to play their style of rugby and limiting the number of penalties conceded. I have no doubt about that. It is only one aspect of what makes a captain, but in the context of a Rugby World Cup, it is key. It is important that captains are highly respected not only by their teammates, but by referees too.

In Dupont (France), Sexton (Ireland) and Kolisi (South Africa) – should he make it – there is no doubt that the three tournament favourites, in my opinion, have excellent captains who enjoy the overwhelming support of their peers and are excellent rugby players.

Of the three, Sexton is the one most likely to overstep with referees if Ireland are placed under severe pressure. He does tend to berate them during a game, shouting instructions their way, and this has the potential to backfire. Often the referees have to ask him to calm down, and that is not something that will help Ireland's cause.

We saw a clear sign of that in Leinster's Champions Cup defeat to La Rochelle this year. Sexton, the Leinster captain, was injured and watched the match from the dugout, and his verbal attack on South African referee Jaco Peyper in the aftermath made headlines for all the wrong reasons. There will undoubtedly be a huge spotlight on how he treats referees in France, should he escape World Rugby punishment and get there.

The winning approach, as the previous editions have shown us, is always to treat referees with respect. Dupont is mild-mannered and doesn't seem to lose his cool at all, while Siya certainly doesn't.

In appointing a captain, all coaches will look for a figure who can remain level-headed and composed in the most trying situations without letting the standard of his own performance drop. World Cups provide so many heated moments that test the emotional maturity and resilience of a captain, and he must have the mental capacity to get his team through those situations while always fulfilling his role as a player, too.

It is not for everybody. Yes, you have the constant communication making its way from the coaching box to the field, but in the cauldron and heat of battle it is the captain who runs the ship and needs to say and do the right things at the right time.

They are natural leaders, and their leadership qualities make them stand out at their clubs, franchises and at training. It's not that they're more serious about rugby; they've just got a presence and a calmness about them that makes their teammates feel safe and valued. They are the type of figure who is likely to have been head boy at high school, and they have the leadership tools to succeed in life long after rugby.

The perfect captain does not struggle under the weight of responsibility, and does not panic. He remains calm, and has the ability to pass relevant information from the referee to his teammates and vice versa.

Above all, he must have a sound relationship of complete trust and understanding with his head coach. If a captain decides to turn down three points and kick for the corner because he feels the momentum is with his side, he must be able to do that with the backing of his coach. After all, the captain is the one on the field with a sense of how both sides are faring. That is definitely the kind of relationship we have seen between Kolisi, Nienaber and Erasmus.

It would be devastating if Kolisi was unable to lead the Springbok title defence in France, but if he doesn't, the team can at least take comfort in the fact that he has helped to build a solid leadership base over the past five years. Kolisi is the man in charge, but his selfless and inclusive leadership style has empowered those around him.

These days, teams have leaders throughout. There is the line-out general who makes the jumping and throwing calls. The scrummaging leader – often the hooker – will issue instructions in terms of whether to look for a double shove or to wheel the scrum, for example. He will speak to the captain and alert him to how the scrum battle is unfolding and where there might be opportunities to gain an advantage.

There will be defensive leaders in the side too, who make sure everyone is where they need to be in executing the system. That responsibility often falls to the No. 8 for the forwards and the outside centre for the backs. Then you have the halfbacks, who run the game and take key decisions throughout.

A captain will always have other leaders around him, and this is an area where Kolisi has been exceptional. He is collaborative and continually asks questions, seeking advice from those with whom he is sharing the battlefield. You cannot be a selfish person if you're captain, and Siya is definitely not selfish.

Because of how Kolisi has facilitated an environment

of inclusivity and shared input, even if he is ruled out, the Springboks will be able to keep that consistency in France. Whether it was Pollard, Am or Etzebeth captaining, the way the Springboks operated on the field of play would not change drastically.

Still, they would far rather have Kolisi leading them. In so many ways, he is irreplaceable.

10
The matches that will shape France 2023

The special thing about the 2023 Rugby World Cup is that on any given day, any of the top eight or nine teams in the world would back themselves to beat any other.

There are still clear favourites, of course, and there will be in every match, but the northern hemisphere has closed the gap on the southern hemisphere so much that anything can happen.

The nature of the draw means the top teams in the world – Ireland, France, New Zealand and South Africa – are all on a collision course for the quarterfinals. Those sides are all in Pool A and Pool B, which means there will be blockbuster clashes with huge ramifications from the very first match of the competition on 8 September, in which France take on the All Blacks at Stade de France in Paris.

If you go back to the 1995 World Cup, where the All

Blacks thrashed Japan 145-17 in Bloemfontein, you can see how much things have changed. There was such a huge disparity back then between the so-called minor nations and the leading sides. But in 2022, Japan played against New Zealand at home and were in it until the last 15 minutes or so. In the end, they lost 38-31.

The game has grown and there have been massive improvements that have seen upsets along the way. The Springboks had their own taste of what can happen when things go wrong at a World Cup when they were famously beaten by the Japanese in Brighton in 2015.

Even if you look at the likes of Samoa, Fiji, Italy and Tonga – the sides ranked from No. 12 to No. 15 in the world – they have also made big strides. Italy's games in the Six Nations have become a lot closer and the teams from the Pacific Islands have unbelievable athletes, so this World Cup is as much about these sides as it is the favourites.

Hopefully we will see tight games between the heavy-weight nations and the minnows, which would be a really good thing. Over the last few years, World Rugby has ensured the smaller nations play against the top sides far more regularly, and I think the organisation should be applauded for driving that. Georgia, for example, are now playing at least one or two Tests a year against a top-10 team, and that can only benefit their rugby and raise the standard of the game.

If we look at the four pools, they will deliver several

intriguing encounters. Some are more clear-cut than others, but every pool has its own dynamic and will deliver fixtures that determine the shape of the whole tournament.

Pool A
FRANCE, NEW ZEALAND, ITALY, URUGUAY, NAMIBIA

France v New Zealand
8 September, Stade de France (Paris)

The opening game between France and the All Blacks could easily be a World Cup final. The All Blacks are historically the best-performing side the game has seen and are always fancied at World Cups, while France must be considered one of the tournament favourites given the rugby they are playing and the fact that they are hosts.

It is a huge fixture that will ultimately determine who tops the pool going into the quarterfinals, and that makes it a game of massive interest for the defending champion Springboks.

Because of the way Rassie Erasmus and Jacques Nienaber think, I am certain they will enter the World Cup with a preferred quarterfinal opponent already in mind. It is out of their hands, of course, but they will be watching this game very closely.

Would the Springboks like to play against their old

rivals New Zealand in the quarters, or would they prefer to play against France? I haven't spoken to them and I have no idea who they would rather draw, but if I had to guess I think they would prefer to avoid France.

Whoever wins this game will almost certainly finish top of Pool A and play against the side that finishes second in Pool B, which would be one of South Africa, Ireland or Scotland.

The Boks have to focus on their own fixtures and cannot pay too much attention to what is happening in the other pool, but Rassie and Jacques will have a preferred knockout opponent and they will know that playing against France in front of their own crowd with a referee under immense pressure will be tough.

My gut feeling is that the Boks would rather play the All Blacks and avoid the host nation, who will have all the momentum behind them. And by that logic, the Boks will want France to win this match. That would leave them fully focused on beating Scotland and Ireland in Pool B, securing top spot and banking a quarterfinal against the All Blacks.

There is no easy route for South Africa, and their quarterfinal promises to be significantly tougher than their semifinal, but this is the way I think they would prefer to progress.

The Springboks have won a World Cup before after losing a pool game – they did it in 2019 – so that won't be of much concern to Rassie and Jacques. In fact, I'd go as far as saying the Boks would rather play the All Blacks in the quarterfinals, even if it meant they were beaten by one of Ireland or Scotland before that.

Make no mistake, the Springboks will still want to beat every team in front of them, but if losing a pool game means they avoid France, that wouldn't be a disaster. Far from it.

France are my favourites to win this game, mainly because of the momentum they have built up over the last two years and their often-impenetrable defensive structure. They have shown an incredible ability to turn it on when they need to, and there are few bigger occasions than a World Cup opener against the three-time champion All Blacks.

There is huge belief both within and accompanying this French side, and with New Zealand coming into the game away from home and after a difficult preparation period, it all points to a France win.

The All Blacks simply don't have the dominance they once had, certainly not in the tight five, and I think France are now matching the southern hemisphere physicality of times past.

At every World Cup before this, France would have entered a clash against the All Blacks – whether in the pool stages or in the knockouts – as underdogs, but I don't think they will feel like that this time.

For the All Blacks not to go into a World Cup as

favourites will be very unusual given their dominance of the game, but even if they lose this one they will still have a major role to play as the tournament unfolds. If they do beat France, it will be a massive statement.

Unfortunately, this game ultimately determines Pool A, even though nine other fixtures follow. If there were to be an upset in what seems a pretty straightforward pool to predict, it would probably come in the form of Italy landing a shock win against France or New Zealand. But that just isn't going to happen. It's a step too far for them.

If Italy were on the other side of the draw and in a pool with one of England, Australia, Argentina or Wales, for example, they would perhaps be in with a shot. But they have had the most rotten luck – like Scotland in Pool B – and have the most difficult, and almost impossible, path to the knockouts.

You simply can't see France slipping up in their own World Cup against Italy, even though Italy held them close in the 2023 Six Nations when they went down 29-24 in Rome. There will no doubt be some entertaining rugby along the way, but ultimately the tournament opener will determine this pool.

Despite that, it is a fantastic way to kick off the competition and set the tone for the heavyweight clashes to follow.

Pool B
SOUTH AFRICA, IRELAND, SCOTLAND, TONGA, ROMANIA

This is a far more complex pool, and it's down to the fact that Ireland and South Africa have Scotland to contend with too. There is no other pool with a more challenging third-seeded participant than this, with Scotland solidifying their position as No. 5 in the world in the build-up. There is no way Ireland or the Boks can go into their respective fixtures against the Scottish team with a casual attitude.

South Africa v Scotland
10 September, Stade Vélodrome (Marseille)

This is the Springboks' first match in their title defence, and such an important one to win. If they slip up here, they will need to beat Ireland later in the pool to secure their place in the playoffs, and the pressure will be immense.

The Springboks have never been knocked out of a World Cup in the group stages, but defeat in their first game in France would make that a real possibility. There is so much riding on this one.

By the time the game kicks off, the Boks will know who won between France and New Zealand, but that will have no bearing on what is undeniably their 2023 World Cup banana peel.

If Scotland win this, it throws the pool wide open

and also has a huge impact on Ireland, who might need victories over Scotland and the Boks to secure their qualification.

I have South Africa as favourites in this match, but far stranger things have happened in World Cup rugby, and a Scotland victory has the potential to open a can of worms that both the Boks and Ireland could do without.

The huge red flag for this game from a South African point of view is the increased physicality of the Scots, who can now hold their own against anyone in the world. They have a powerful front row, decent lock forwards, solid ball-carrying loose forwards and a backline that displays more natural strength than any Scottish lineup before it.

There is a huge resurgence happening in Scottish rugby. If you look at their backline, where you have the likes of Duhan van der Merwe, Kyle Steyn, Huw Jones and Sione Tuipulotu, you see big, strong guys with huge southern hemisphere influence. If you throw the highly skilled Finn Russell into that mix as the conductor and give him a bit of front-foot ball, they become formidable.

I still can't see Scotland winning though, and I believe South Africa's physicality is going to be too overwhelming for them, but it remains a massive game for both sides. My gut feel is that there won't be more than 10 points in it but that the Springboks will get over the line – even if it isn't pretty.

South Africa v Ireland
23 September, Stade de France (Paris)

This really is *the* fixture of Pool B, and one that I believe will determine which side finishes top. If everything goes according to prediction, then Ireland and South Africa will be too good for Scotland and this fixture will determine who wins Pool B.

Regardless of the outcome of their first match against Scotland, the Springboks will have to be at their best for this one. The only way the Boks can guarantee their path to the knockouts is by beating both Scotland and Ireland, because victory over Scotland and defeat to Ireland could leave them at mathematical risk of being eliminated if Scotland beat Ireland after that. It has the potential to get messy, so the Boks can never relax in their pool.

This match will be an absolute cracker and is as big a game as France v New Zealand in the opener. For the neutral observer it is a fascinating pool, and this is its marquee fixture.

There are intriguing battles all over the park, and while it could be a kick-heavy contest, potentially watching Johnny Sexton and Handré Pollard exchange blows and the Irish trying to match the Springbok physicality will be worth the price of admission on their own.

Ireland, remember, boast the URC winners in Munster, who knocked over the heavily fancied Stormers in the 2023 Cape Town final. When you consider that

Munster were only the third highest-ranked Irish side on the URC log behind Ulster and Leinster, then this clash is an absolute headliner. I can't wait for it.

It is a more difficult game to predict than France v New Zealand, and really could go either way. But if the Springboks show up and tick all their boxes, they should have enough to secure another win.

Much of it comes down to how the match is refereed, but if the Boks get a fair crack there I reckon they will back themselves. Even if they do lose the match, however, I believe South Africa will still finish second and move on to the quarterfinals.

Ireland v Scotland
7 October, Stade de France (Paris)

Ireland will certainly be favourites for this game as the top-ranked side in the world, but Scotland aren't miles away for all the reasons I gave above in relation to their fixture against South Africa.

The teams will know exactly where the pool stands, as they will both have played the Springboks by this stage, so this will almost certainly be a do-or-die contest for at least one of them.

But regardless of what happens in their clash against the Boks, Ireland will still enter this one believing they will be too strong for their Celtic rivals.

Leinster, in my opinion, is the top side in Europe

despite falling short again in the URC and the Champions Cup in 2023, and they feed Ireland with the bulk of its national team. Ireland know their system and their game plan so well, and there is so much continuity feeding through from their professional franchises.

They are about as prepared as a side could possibly be heading into a World Cup, and probably three or four years ahead of Scotland in terms of team development. Even so, this fixture also has the potential to leave us on the edge of our seats.

It's going to be a fantastic game, and Scotland must believe they have the goods to pull off an upset that could rock the entire competition.

Pool C
WALES, AUSTRALIA, FIJI, GEORGIA, PORTUGAL

This half of the draw does not have the quality of the title contenders in pools A and B, but it is perhaps even more intriguing in light of the upsets that could be on the cards.

With Wales struggling, Fiji and Georgia will be eyeing that fixture as their way of progressing. Fiji are the most likely to ruffle feathers, in my opinion, but Georgia have shown amazing growth in recent years and have a solid scrum that could make them an uncomfortable team to play against. I still think, though, that Australia and Wales will have too much for Georgia.

Wales v Fiji
10 September, Nouveau Stade de Bordeaux (Bordeaux)

This is the game where I think we could see a real upset. Fiji have improved their scrummaging and maul defence tremendously, and if they are able to showcase those talents against Wales this will be close.

Much of that improvement came under New Zealander Vern Cotter, who suddenly resigned as head coach in February 2023. Cotter took Scotland to the World Cup quarterfinals in 2015, when they lost to Australia in a cloud of refereeing controversy, and he did great work for Fiji.

When playing against a side such as Fiji, you cannot allow the game to get loose because they have so many strong, fast, mobile players who can get a pass away that could break the game open. You have to make them maul and scrum, so if they arrive in France improved in those departments, they could be a handful.

I'm not sure Wales have the tight five to really dominate Fiji in that space, so I'm viewing this as a great opportunity for Fiji to make a play at the tournament. It would be a huge upset, yes, but when you look at where Wales are, it would not be that surprising.

Fiji, of course, have benefited hugely from having Fijian Drua competing in Super Rugby Pacific, even if results have not always gone their way. Teams such as South Africa, Ireland, France and New Zealand would have the ability to contain Fiji because they would dominate the set piece and battle up front to win a stream of penalties, but I don't think we can say the same for Wales. They don't have the players with the physical prowess of the top sides.

Australia v Fiji
17 September – Stade Geoffroy-Guichard (St Étienne)

While I also don't believe Australia have the pack of forwards to completely take Fiji out the game, I think they will have the momentum going into this World Cup with Eddie Jones on board as coach.

Because they play against the Fijians so often in Super Rugby Pacific, they are well aware of the dangers the islanders can present. It might be closer than they would like, but I think the Wallabies will get over the line and avoid an upset here. Wales, though, have not had that constant exposure to the unique Fijian style and improved physicality.

Australia v Wales
24 September, Parc Olympique Lyonnais (Décines-Charpieu)

This should be the two top seeds in the pool going at it for top spot. If Wales have lost to Fiji, however, then this could be a ding-dong battle of the most desperate proportions.

Both sides have made late coaching changes heading into the tournament, and if either of them has slipped up against the Fijians, this could be a straight shootout.

I think Australia should win it with Jones at the helm, given his track record of taking teams far in World Cups. If Japan under Jones could beat South Africa at the 2015 World Cup, for example, then I think Australia under Jones should get past an average Welsh outfit.

I have Australia qualifying top of this pool undefeated, with Fiji possibly sneaking through with an upset win over the 2019 semifinalists, Wales.

Pool D
ENGLAND, JAPAN, ARGENTINA, SAMOA, CHILE

This is such an interesting pool, and much of that is down to the dark horse, Japan, who have a very good coaching team under Jamie Joseph and former New Zealand fly half Tony Brown. They have done a fantastic job and there is a lot of continuity.

Japanese rugby has been strengthened by the South Africans, New Zealanders and Australians who have relocated there, and that has transformed a set piece that in the past struggled due to the absence of a strong tight five.

Japan are proving to be a difficult team to beat, and in a pool that also includes England and Argentina, the

2019 quarterfinalists could be a severe disruption. This pool is wide open.

England v Argentina
9 September, Stade Vélodrome (Marseille)

Argentina, for me, are the favourites in the pool. It might seem like a bold thing to say, but I think England and Japan probably have an equal chance of making it through to the quarterfinals.

I believe Argentina will win this game, and it's simply down to the fact that England don't have the team. They might have a coach in Steve Borthwick whom the players will believe in and play for, but you have to ask yourself: where are England's world-class players? I don't believe they have them. How many English players would make a World XV right now? None, in my view.

Argentina, meanwhile, have players scattered across Europe who are among the best at their respective franchises or clubs. They also have an annual examination of their skills in the Rugby Championship against South Africa, New Zealand and Australia, and I think the improvement they have shown there speaks volumes about their development. Under coach Michael Cheika and captain Julián Montoya, they have become the real deal.

I can guarantee that the crowd for this match will be firmly behind Argentina, and every Frenchman in attendance will want England to lose. I cannot emphasise enough how strongly the French feel about supporting anybody who plays against England, and given everything we have said about the pressures on referees in crunch matches such as this, I believe that works even more in Argentina's favour.

When I was coaching Italy from 2007 to 2011, and after games in the Six Nations, it was amazing how many times our opposition would encourage us to go out and beat England in our next match. The English, for whatever reason, are not a popular side among their northern hemisphere peers, and that applies to the French more than anyone.

This prediction might leave English supporters thinking I am off my head, but I don't think it is that far-fetched. Argentina beat Eddie Jones's England 30-29 at Twickenham the last time the sides met, after all. Everyone said that result happened because England were no longer playing for Jones, but I think it was because Argentina are a very good side. If England are not at the top of their game for this one, they could be in for another shock.

England v Japan
17 September, Allianz Riviera (Nice)

Given everything I have said above, this has the potential to be a make-or-break game for England, and when sides are under pressure, strange things can happen.

Japan will be going flat out here and they will believe that if they can hold New Zealand for the bulk of a Test match, as they did in 2022, they can do even better against an England side that has significantly less quality.

They won't enter this with any fear, and their coaching group have given them the organisation and structure to mount a challenge. I still have England winning this one, but I think it will be tight.

Japan v Argentina
8 October – Stade de la Beaujoire (Nantes)

This is the final game in the pool and is also likely to be very close. When I talk about the likes of Scotland and Italy being unlucky that they are not on this side of the draw, I think Japan have benefited. There is a gilt-edged opportunity for them to progress, and even if they lose against England they could have one last crack at making the playoffs with victory in this one.

It really would be a sensational effort if they were able to do that in back-to-back World Cups, and it would be confirmation of the sustained growth and improvement in the region. Both teams will have everything to play for, and it promises to be an intriguing contest.

All four pools have tantalising fixtures, and it is only Pool A that the two qualifiers – France and New Zealand – are all but certain.

Pool B should see South Africa and Ireland progress, on paper at least, but Scotland will have their say in that.

Then, Fiji could throw the cat among the pigeons with Australia and Wales in Pool C, while Pool D is wide open.

It would also be foolish to write off Georgia in Pool C. People forget that in 2022 Georgia beat Wales 13-12, and the hard truth for Warren Gatland's team is that they have not shown improvement since that Test. Upsets happen, and the top-tier teams can no longer ignore those ranked outside the top 10.

Let the games begin!

11
All it takes is a moment

They are the moments we remember forever. They are replayed countless times – in television advertisements, documentaries, and on social media – reminding us of how much it hurts to lose and how good it feels to win.

Sometimes in rugby, all the preparation in the world is undone by one moment of sheer individual brilliance. Sometimes, the tactics and game plans take a back seat, and in one moment of excellence or misfortune a game is won or lost.

We have seen this so many times at World Cups. You only have to look at the number of finals and playoff matches that have been decided by a drop goal, for example, to understand how a single moment can define a tournament.

It is not only the drop goals. It can be the bounce of a ball, a refereeing decision, a sidestep or a sublime no-look pass that makes history. These are the moments in time that can be the difference between a World Cup win and a loss.

Think about the moment in 1995 when France's Abdelatif Benazzi had a try disallowed in the semifinal against the Springboks in Durban. We have spoken about that moment already, and if the decision had gone the other way – as it so easily could have – there would have been no Mandela Miracle.

No movies would have been made and no books would have been written about how the Springboks pulled off the unthinkable to unite a nation and forge a new way forward of togetherness. The course of rugby as we know it would look very different. One moment, one decision changed everything. A blade of grass.

Very few people remember that in the 1995 World Cup final, the All Blacks had a fantastic opportunity just outside the Springbok 22-metre area deep into the second half. Andrew Mehrtens went back into the pocket and tried a drop goal. He was under a lot of pressure from a charging Joost van der Westhuizen, and if you go back and look at that moment you'll see that Joost was offside by a mile. He was not behind the last man's feet, but there were no TMOs in those days and the referee didn't see it.

Mehrtens missed, the game went to extra time and

Joel Stransky kicked a drop goal that made his career. On another day, the referee could have penalised Joost, and Mehrtens – the best kicker in the world at the time – would have had an easy shot at goal to win his side the World Cup.

I have told the story of how we got Jannie de Beer to kick those drop goals for us at the World Cup in 1999, and it was nothing short of exceptional to see him land five in a row against England in the Paris quarterfinal. He didn't miss one, knocking them out so comfortably and scoring 15 points in less than 20 minutes. We had never done anything like that before, so there was no way it could have been predicted by England.

The irony, of course, is that it was a drop goal that spelt the end of our participation at that year's tournament, too. I remember saying to Joost – my captain – before that semifinal in London that the Wallabies would have plans to counter our drop kick strategy, given what had transpired in the quarterfinal.

They were going to put as much pressure as possible on Jannie, which meant the first and second defenders at the rucks would be setting off out of their blocks as fast as they could to close down the space. It opened a massive opportunity for Joost to throw the dummy, duck his head and break. If that break was in the Australian 22-metre area, I believed we'd have an opportunity to score a try.

With the game in the balance and time running out, Joost did exactly that. He threw a dummy just outside the 22, beating both of their defenders, and went through the gap. The closest player to him was Os du Randt.

Joost drew the fullback and made the pass to Os, but Wallabies scrum half George Gregan was covering. The size difference meant Gregan couldn't tackle Os front-on, but unfortunately for us, Os had the ball under the wrong arm. A chasing Gregan dived at the ball, essentially tackling it out of Os's hand, and just five metres from the line he knocked on.

It was such a fantastic opportunity to win that match right there, before extra time. If we had scored and converted, we would have been four or five points ahead with virtually no time left, and how different things could have been for us.

People don't remember that, but boy, do they remember Stephen Larkham's drop goal! It was an extraordinary feat, and to this day I still think he was trying to kick the ball dead to give the Wallabies territorial dominance. I spoke to their coach Rod Macqueen afterwards, and that was their message during those crucial minutes.

Larkham kicked it as hard as he could, hoping the ball would either go dead or – by some miracle – through the uprights. We all know what happened next. It was a one-in-a-hundred chance, and he took it. Fair play to him.

I still find myself replaying that game in my head, all these years later. Again, there were so many little moments that, had they gone differently, could have changed everything.

The penalty Jannie kicked on the stroke of full-time, in a swirling wind and from miles out to the right, was one of them. It had no bearing on the final result, as it turned out, but it was the most extraordinary kick. There was so much pressure on him, but it went straight through the poles and never looked like missing.

These are the incredible moments of pressure that a Rugby World Cup dishes up, and there is no doubt in my mind that there will be many more in 2023. It is what makes knockout rugby so unbelievably watchable.

The World Cup final in 2003 is another great example. It was a very tight game which South Africa's André Watson was refereeing. I remember being quite confused, because even though the England pack were stronger, Watson gave Australia several penalties when they were under the pump that I felt kept them in the game.

The match was in the balance and went to extra time with the scoreline 14-14 after 80 minutes. The difference proved to be a moment of brilliance from Jonny Wilkinson.

In the 100th minute of that epic battle, with the scores tied at 17-17, Wilkinson shaped onto his weaker right foot and kicked a drop goal that gave England their first and only World Cup title and the greatest moment in their rugby history.

It was another case of a drop goal making and breaking a game, taking the referee out of the equation. It was about a player – Wilkinson, in this case – being able to handle the huge weight on his shoulders, and delivering.

In 2007, when the Springboks won under Jake White, there was a moment in the final when numerous television replays sought to determine whether England wing Mark Cueto had scored a try in the left corner.

England were six points adrift at that stage with the bulk of the second half still to play, but you could clearly see that Cueto's boot had touched the whitewash before the ball was grounded. It was a matter of centimetres, and Danie Rossouw's tackle proved to be just enough for the Boks.

Had there not been the technology and the TMO to make that decision, who knows what would have happened? It would have been very easy, I think, for that try to have been given.

It was a devastating moment for England and, when the call didn't go their way, it went a long way towards extinguishing their chances. The Boks went on to win the match quite comfortably.

In 2011, the Springboks went into their World Cup

quarterfinal without a clear drop goal strategy, and it came back to haunt them.

The Boks were convinced they were strong enough to knock over the Wallabies by scoring tries and getting penalties, but the problem was that referee Bryce Lawrence didn't award any penalties to South Africa.

By the end of the game, the Springboks had spent around 25 minutes in the Australian half, and while Morné Steyn did kick one spontaneous drop goal to give the Boks the lead for the first time in the game on the hour mark, I always felt the Boks would have come out on the right side of that contest had Steyn taken that option more regularly in that game.

Sometimes you get situations where the referee is not giving you the benefit of the doubt, and a drop goal is a way in which an attacking team can put points on the board without relying on those penalty calls. Drop goals have played such a pivotal role in so many key Rugby World Cup games, and I think every team now understands their value.

In that year's World Cup final between New Zealand and France, there was also a vital kick for the All Blacks' Stephen Donald, his country's fourth-choice fly half. Imagine being out fishing and getting a phone call, mid-tournament, calling you up! It was a remarkable story, and when he kicked that second-half penalty it was his moment. The All Blacks won 8-7.

I still believe that Dan Carter's drop goal against the

Springboks in the semifinal, off the top of a line-out they stole, was the difference in that game. The drop came when the All Blacks were down to 14 men with Jerome Kaino off the field, and they won the match 20-18.

Carter was such a superb rugby player at the peak of his game and he was always so capable of identifying those moments and delivering the goods. In a really tight game, Carter showed great understanding of what was required in taking that option, at that moment.

There were no decisive drop goals in 2019 but there were certainly moments of individual brilliance, and South African fans will never forget the dazzling skills that defined the final against England.

There was Malcolm Marx's pass that released Makazole Mapimpi, who then executed a perfect chip that Lukhanyo Am gathered expertly. Then, there was the no-look pass from Am straight back to Mapimpi, whose try sent vibrations across a celebrating South Africa. It was the most perfect Springbok moment and it was made possible by every single player performing his role perfectly. These were small windows of opportunity that were exploited by the Springboks in an instant, and it wasn't just one man who did it but a combination of players.

It was exactly the same with Cheslin Kolbe's try seven minutes later. Marx's tackle allowed Am to protect the ball on the ground, and he was very clever in giving

Pieter-Steph du Toit the time to pick it up and throw the pass. Kolbe did the rest, brilliantly wrong footing Owen Farrell to pieces, and the rest is history.

It was instantaneous excellence, in a brief moment, that would have seismic consequences. It's the ability to exploit an opportunity and not make a mistake when the stakes are at their highest, and I think the Springboks did exactly that with both of their tries in the 2019 final.

Looking forward to 2023, what individual brilliance can we expect to see? The very nature of these moments means they are impossible to predict, but there are certain teams and players that you just know have it in their locker. We have seen that X factor from the likes of Kurt-Lee Arendse and Manie Libbok at both franchise and international level in recent seasons, for example, and every team will have guys who can blow a game wide open.

These are the players who can do things outstandingly well under a level of pressure that might be suffocating for others. In extremely tight games – and there will be many of those at Rugby World Cup 2023 – they are the moments in time that decide outcomes and shape history.

Let's take a closer look at who I think those players could be, again going through our obvious title-contending teams.

France
Antoine Dupont and Romain Ntamack

These two, the halfbacks, are critical to taking France deep into this competition. They are superb players and they will drive the French machine. Dupont is nerveless, and like Ntamack can knock over a cheeky drop goal if the situation dictates.

Dupont is the complete player and the leader of this French outfit. He could make a decisive tackle or throw a world-class pass, and you expect him to be involved in most things France do well.

Ireland
Johnny Sexton

Sexton, if available, is critical to Ireland's World Cup charge, not only because of his creativity and ability to take the ball to the line, but because of his goalkicking.

Sexton has nailed so many match-deciding kicks over his Leinster, Ireland and British & Irish Lions career, and he is exactly the man you want in such defining moments.

He also has the drop goal in his locker and very impressive rugby intelligence, so he will be able to identify exactly when it could be on. Hopefully, for Ireland's sake, he will return to full fitness in time and make those vital decisions in massive games.

South Africa
Handré Pollard and Lukhanyo Am

There is a lot of hype around Manie Libbok being a No. 10 option for the Boks going into this World Cup, but Pollard has the experience and ability to win pressure games. He remains calm in the tensest examinations of mental strength, and delivers the goods. His performance in the 2019 semifinal against Wales is an example of that, and I think he will be crucial again in those games of fine margins.

Am, in the blink of an eye, will take the right decision. He has done it countless times, and it is no wonder so many view him as the best No. 13 in the world. He has a vision that others simply don't possess, and you can't coach that. Am will see something that nobody else does, and by the time he has executed, it'll be too late for the opposition to stop it.

He might not kick a drop goal but Am will hold onto the ball for a split-second longer to open up space, deliver an audacious offload or even chip ahead to create something out of nothing. His timing is impeccable.

New Zealand
Richie Mo'unga and Will Jordan

Mo'unga and Jordan are very different players but both have the ability to do extraordinary things on a rugby field. The All Blacks look to have settled on Mo'unga as their fly half, and he always seems to make the right decision about whether to kick, run or pass.

I expect the All Blacks to come off second best in the forwards battle against the best teams in the competition, but they will take comfort in having a gamebreaker like Mo'unga pulling the strings. He can certainly spark a moment of magic for them.

Jordan, meanwhile, has an incredible try-scoring ability and rugby instinct. When he is on the ball, there is always the feeling that something special is about to happen.

Scotland

Finn Russell

We know that Scotland have a newfound physical strength to their backline, but nobody in their ranks possesses more of a gamebreaking ability than Russell. We saw him come very close to sparking the British & Irish Lions to a series win over the Springboks in 2021, and he has been influencing matches like that for years.

Russell has a great appreciation of where his runners are, and more often than not he picks the right one. He is also a fearless playmaker, and whether it be with a cross kick or a high-risk pass, he is prepared to roll the dice. It can backfire, but it can also ignite those moments that come out of nothing and result in a try.

Argentina
Emiliano Boffelli

Playing his rugby at Edinburgh in the URC, Boffelli was Argentina's hero in their famous 30-29 victory over England at Twickenham in 2022. He scored 25 points that day. He was Argentina's starting fullback at the 2019 World Cup but has since been shifted to the wing, where his pace and linebreaking ability have made him a force.

Boffelli is also tasked with goalkicking, and he has been largely solid in that department. That, combined with his natural attacking prowess, makes him the most likely of the Argentineans to deliver a moment of magic in France.

Australia
Quade Cooper

The Wallabies have not yet settled on their World Cup fly half, but if we're talking about guys who are natural visionaries on a rugby field, I think Cooper is certainly one of them. Australia don't really have much else going for them in that department, which is precisely why Cooper will be such an attractive option for Eddie Jones in France.

England
Owen Farrell

I don't believe England will be title contenders in 2023,

but in Farrell they at least have an ice-cool goalkicker who will never be flustered. Like Johnny Sexton, he has done it before on the biggest stages at club and international level.

He has the solidity of a Handré Pollard. There is nothing too spectacular, but in a huge game he can deliver a flawless kicking performance, and that so often gets you over the line in a World Cup knockout affair.

Wales

Dan Biggar

Biggar might not even be picked as the first-choice No. 10 for Wales at the World Cup, but he will be very hard to ignore. He was the British & Irish Lions' first-choice fly half under Warren Gatland on their South African tour, and over the years we have seen him kick conversions, penalties and drop goals to win games all over the world.

Biggar also has the World Cup experience – he came close to playing in the 2019 final – and that is something the struggling Welsh side will need desperately. If anyone can ignite Wales in France, it is surely Biggar.

These are the players coaches will be looking at to take instantaneous decisions that win games. Every team at Rugby World Cup 2023 will have their own systems, frameworks and game plans that will be their recipe for success.

We know that the Springboks, Ireland, France and New Zealand are the favourites to go the distance, even if they are all lumped on the same side of the draw. The systems they have – and the coaching and playing personnel to supplement those systems – have provided us with enough clues to predict the real contenders.

But time and time again in this tournament, matches have been won or lost in a single moment. Coaches can only do so much. Sometimes, it comes down to one player making a call. And sometimes, that call defines greatness.

12
Where to next?

The stage is set, and for seven weeks between 8 September and 28 October we will sit back and enjoy a feast of rugby. The World Cup is the pinnacle of our great sport, and I firmly believe that given everything we have discussed – how open this competition is, how the north has closed the gap on the south, and the rise of Ireland and France – this will be the most entertaining, intriguing tournament yet.

But where to beyond 2023?

The game is in a healthy space, and while there are obvious concerns and unanswered questions about its future, we can confidently say it is moving in the right direction. That is certainly the case in South Africa, where hopefully the age of private equity will soon see money flowing into our top franchises and even our mother body, SA Rugby.

We have already seen that benefit at the Sharks through their acquisition by the US consortium MVM Holdings, and that sort of external investment will be crucial in helping South Africa to keep its best players operating within its own system, as has been the case in Ireland.

The appetite for our game remains incredibly strong. On Saturdays, I am always amazed when we see thousands of spectators watching schoolboy rugby, passionately cheering on their children, classmates or alma mater.

The strength of South Africa's schoolboy rugby is always such a strong reminder for me of the power of this game. No other country in the world has a school system like ours, and it should be treasured. As long as kids are growing up wanting to play the game and become Springboks, rugby will always be in a strong position.

There has been so much disruption in the game in recent years, especially in South Africa where the decision to move on from Super Rugby raised eyebrows and left an uneasy feeling for many fans. I believe it was the correct move. The game is thriving in Europe, and SA Rugby's decision to align itself with the United Rugby Championship and European Cup competitions was a masterstroke.

There will always be those who miss the thrill of

playing against the New Zealand franchises in Super Rugby, but in terms of long-term financial and commercial success, it was the way to go. About 80 per cent of rugby's global revenue comes from the northern hemisphere, so South Africa has attached itself to a sound, lucrative model. The financial gains might not come immediately – South African franchises, through SARU, have had to buy their way into the URC and Europe – but aligning ourselves with the euro and the pound is a smart move.

There is still the possibility of the Springboks joining the Six Nations, too, which would further entrench South Africa's place in Europe. The Six Nations is a historic competition with a tribal essence to it, and entire nations get behind their teams. It's hugely popular and followed by a tremendous number of supporters, so from a financial point of view it is an attractive option.

In terms of playing standards, South Africa have benefited immensely from playing against New Zealand and Australia in the past, but we mustn't forget that they have benefited from playing us, too. An expansion into a Seven Nations, if you will, would also ensure that every team plays three games at home and three away, which would tidy up the format and give the competing sides equal footing in that sense.

South Africa's involvement would mean it would no longer be an exclusively European competition, but it would be fair in terms of scheduling. With the viewing figures the Springboks bring, I think expansion of the Six Nations could potentially be as exciting for Europe as it would be for South Africa.

South African teams have made their mark with a really good initial showing in the URC, driven by the Stormers. On the domestic front, it might take franchises four or five years to get to a place where they can compete equally in the URC and European Champions Cup, but I think they are in there for the long run.

SA Rugby is committed to the Springboks playing in the Rugby Championship until the end of 2025, but if a move into the Six Nations follows then hopefully – after a few seasons of our franchises playing in the URC and Champions Cup – the European countries will have softened somewhat in any hostility that might accompany a Springbok inclusion.

My feeling is that it would be great for international rugby and that the Springboks would bring strength and diversity, as well as the viewership figures, to make the Six Nations the premier international rugby competition short of the World Cup itself.

Over the past two seasons we have seen great crowds watching South African sides in the URC, particularly the Stormers, and when you factor in the South African television viewership, I believe Europe will see the value in further accommodating the Springboks.

If SA Rugby solidifies its administrative setup, where there have been some issues which have caused the

departure of former CEO Jurie Roux, then I believe
that with sound judgement and decision-making South
Africa is perfectly positioned to remain a powerhouse of
the game, regardless of what happens to the Springboks
in France.

Despite all of that, there are concerns elsewhere. I am
very worried about the future of Australian rugby,
and that has nothing to do with their administration.
I just think we are seeing their player pool shrinking,
and it is understandable when you think that they have
Aussie rules football and rugby league to contend with.
Imagine if South Africa's schoolchildren were split
between three variations of the game.

For me, international rugby needs Australian rugby to
be strong. The Wallabies – two-time world champions
– are an integral part of the history of the sport, and
seeing their steady decline over the years has been so
unfortunate. In that sense, I hope the Wallabies can
go deep into the 2023 World Cup – perhaps to a semifinal – and get some support swelling at home.

What is happening in Wales, too, is worrying.
Whenever you have a situation where players and staff
are threatening to down tools, and where payment is
becoming an issue, you know you are not in a good spot.

There are always challenges, but hopefully we'll see
both countries come out stronger on the other side for

the 2027 World Cup in Australia. The 2023 edition will be over in the blink of an eye, and while four years seems a long time to wait for the next one, that is exactly what makes this tournament so prestigious.

My other hope for the game is that we continue to see the growth of the so-called smaller nations. Wouldn't it be fantastic if, by the time we get to the 2031 World Cup in the US, we have an American team that could progress to the knockouts? That might seem like a pipe dream at this stage, but it is the growth the sport needs.

The reason Rugby World Cup 2023 is so exciting is that there are so many teams – as many as eight – who will be backing themselves to go the distance. The rise of France, Ireland and Scotland has thrown the competition wide open, and that is what we need more of in the game.

In football, there is the feeling that anything can happen on any given day, regardless of who is playing. Wouldn't it be wonderful if we had something similar in rugby?

Another area where I think rugby needs to take a long, hard look at itself beyond France 2023 is in its rulebook. If the game is to keep growing, and keep attracting young players and crowds, then it needs to speed up and be as exciting as possible for all involved. For me, there is a real need to re-examine the laws.

We are seeing a trend in the game now where sides have realised that not having the ball enhances their chances of success, and that can't be a good thing.

We have professional defence coaches who improve individual and team defence through the accuracy and specialisation of the 'jackler', the first arriving teammate of a tackler. This has made it statistically too risky to hold onto the ball for more than three to five phases, since there is a tendency to concede a penalty or a turnover after that.

This does not make sense, because rugby is a game that should be played successfully with the ball in hand rather than teams statistically having more chance of success without the ball.

Only Ireland, with their 'box attack' of four runners off the scrum half – two direct and two 'out the back' – have mastered the ability to sustain pace and continuity through multiple-phase play. This has proven to be extremely effective, as they are now ranked No. 1 in the world.

However, this multi-phase game plan also embodies numerous dangerous cleans with the risk of head contact, 'crocodile rolls' and side entries, which can bring penalties and yellow or red cards into play.

How can we use law changes to increase the safety of the players while at the same time creating a game that is attractive and exciting to watch? I don't believe the rugby laws do that, as they stand.

When the Springboks and Wales made the semifinals of Rugby World Cup 2019, they produced a horrible rugby spectacle. There were more than 80 kicks in that game, numerous scrum penalties and almost no backline attack by either team. It was a box-kicking war of attrition between the two 10-metre lines, waged in the hope that the team receiving the ball would make an error.

The Boks had the better pack and an excellent goal kicker that day in Handré Pollard, and to the delight of all South African supporters they won the game 19-16.

Both coaches, Warren Gatland and Rassie Erasmus, understood the way the laws of the game were being refereed and that this would be the most effective way to win. The Boks achieved their goal and went on to win the World Cup with a devastating scrumming display against England, scarcely believable defensive efforts at critical times, and the brilliant use of counterattacking opportunities that produced tries by Makazole Mapimpi and Cheslin Kolbe.

Nothing major has changed in the rugby laws in the four years since, so why should the Boks move away from their winning recipe in 2023? They can still win scrum and maul penalties, and the box kick is still a better option than a poor kick deep downfield or gifting a lineout to the opposition. The Boks can kick penalties to the corner to apply pressure through another driving maul, which brings yellow cards into play for the defending team, or they can attack with impunity using the penalty advantage they get from their powerful scrum and maul. There is no need for South Africa to change their tactics.

But if we take off our Springbok hats for the moment, we could and should debate whether this is the style of rugby that will attract more young players, male and female, to play our great game. Will set piece dominance and more accurate tactical kicking draw more spectators to rugby games and attract more TV viewers? Probably not.

If I was tasked with mapping out the future of rugby to make it as accessible as possible, I would propose the following four changes to the laws. They could be trialled in various national amateur competitions to test whether they make the game safer and more attractive for players, spectators and TV viewers. If they do, they could be applied to the professional game.

1. No direct penalties from scrums, give a free kick instead. No 'scrum again' option either

The team winning the free kick can 'tap and go' from the spot where the scrum was set and not behind their

No. 8's feet. This would have two big benefits.

First, there would be far fewer reset scrums (dangerous for neck injuries and a dreadful waste of time) as the opportunity now would not be to attempt to win a penalty with a double shove but to attack with the ball through the backline. There are 16 forwards involved in the scrum so there would be more space on the field.

Second, it would be very dangerous to give away a scrummaging 'free kick' as the attacking team could immediately 'tap and go', putting 15 of their own players behind the ball on attack. Only seven of the defending team would be able to defend immediately, as all their forwards would be within 10 metres of the 'free kick' and offside.

This would ensure that scrummaging expertise would still be vital and that the shape of the props would remain the same!

2. The defending team can collapse a maul with no penalty

I have yet to see any forward getting injured by a collapsed maul, as it is a slow and reasonably static event. This and the double-shoved scrum are the two areas of the game where the defensive team cannot get to the attacking player controlling the ball because other attacking players are between them and the ball.

In open play, when an attacking player makes contact

with a defensive opponent in front of his own ball carrier, it is a penalty against the attacking team. How does one reconcile this with the maul penalty given against the defensive team when they collapse the maul, despite any number of attacking players being in front of the ball carrier? It is nonsensical.

3. Any kick can be 'marked' if the ball is caught on the full, anywhere on the field

The option for the team catching the ball on the full can be either to 'tap and go' or to choose a scrum from where the ball was kicked.

This would put a stop to the endless box kicks from scrum halves or up-and-unders from fly halves that have become such a big part of the game. If the receiver had a clean catch, 'marked' the ball and had the option of a scrum where it was kicked, this would immediately reduce kicking as an option.

It would also virtually eliminate the inevitable danger of two players clashing in an aerial contest, which still happens regularly. This has been one of the main safety concerns in rugby and this law change would reduce not only the potential of serious injuries but also the blight of yellow and red cards.

It would force teams either to find grass with their kick or to put the ball out and concede the line-out throw to the opposition.

4. Finding touch from a penalty gives the opposition the line-out

Wayne Smith, the highly respected former All Black coach and assistant to Graham Henry in 2011 and Steve Hansen in 2015, who also coached the New Zealand women's team to victory in the Women's Rugby World Cup in 2022, has proposed this simple law change. I agree with it fully.

If a team wins a penalty and chooses to kick it out, the throw-in goes to the opposing team, and the team who kicked it out relinquishes possession. This law change would immediately put an end to the repetitive penalty-kick for touch-collapsed driving maul-penalty-kick for touch-collapsed driving maul-yellow card sequence which has been another main cause of the increase in yellow cards.

Trialling these law changes and analysing the way they affect the game, from both the safety and the entertainment perspective, would be extremely valuable. I believe most rugby supporters and players would like the game to be safer, but that there should also be fewer stoppages and less time-wasting because of scrum resets, yellow/red cards and long TMO deliberations. In my opinion, all of these law changes would contribute towards achieving this.

The one constant in rugby is that it continually evolves. The game today bears very little resemblance to amateur games played in the 1980s, and those games looked nothing like the games played in the 1950s.

My great hope is that our magnificent game of rugby, which emphasises teamwork, unselfishness, commitment, courage, discipline, inclusivity, respect and friendship, will survive and thrive, despite the pressures of professionalism, concussion-related lawsuits and the many other issues it faces.

I have been fortunate enough to have played the game for 30 years in South Africa, England, Italy and France. I have coached rugby for 25 years in France, South Africa and Italy and talked about the game on television for 12 years with my current rugby family, SuperSport.

This beautiful game has been a part of my life for as long as I can remember, and I owe it such a huge debt.

I wish Rugby, my dearest friend, the 'best of luck': 'sterkte' in Afrikaans, 'merde' in French, and 'in bocca al lupo' in Italian. What a wonderful life you have given me.

But before we wrap this up, let's have some fun!

Predicting winners at a World Cup is always a dangerous game; so many curve balls are dished up along the way. But after everything we have discussed in this book, it is only right for me to stick my neck out.

If I had to bet my house on it (and I certainly won't be doing that!) then these are the picks I would make for Rugby World Cup 2023 in France.

Group stages:

Pool A: France 1st, New Zealand 2nd
Pool B: South Africa 1st, Ireland 2nd
Pool C: Australia 1st, Wales 2nd
Pool D: Argentina 1st, England 2nd

Quarterfinals:

France v Ireland
South Africa v New Zealand
Australia v England
Argentina v Wales

Semifinalists:

France v Argentina
South Africa v Australia

The Rugby World Cup 2023 final:

France v South Africa

For me, this would be a dream final, but the Springboks would need to beat Ireland, Scotland, New Zealand and Australia to get there. If they go the distance and become the first nation in the history of the World Cup to lift the Webb Ellis Cup four times, this will surely have been the most difficult path they have ever taken. It is the ultimate test.

Even if I put my bias aside, I still genuinely believe the Springboks have what it takes to win. France and Ireland might be the people's favourites this time around, but under the guidance of Rassie Erasmus and Jacques Nienaber, the Springboks tick all the right boxes. The bulk of this squad have already achieved on the highest, grandest stages the game has to offer – Japan 2019 and in the 2021 British & Irish Lions series – and I reckon they can do it again in 2023.

The Springboks are a championship side, and if they find a way over the line in France they will be considered one of the greatest teams rugby has ever seen.

I can't wait!

2023 RUGBY WORLD CUP POOLS

POOL A
New Zealand
France
Italy
Uruguay
Namibia

POOL B
South Africa
Ireland
Scotland
Tonga
Romania

POOL C
Wales
Australia
Fiji
Georgia
Portugal

POOL D
England
Japan
Argentina
Samoa
Chile

POOL A

France, New Zealand, Italy, Uruguay, Namibia

MATCH DATE		TEAMS PLAYING		STADIUM		RESULTS
8 September 2023		France v New Zealand		Stade de France, Saint-Denis		
9 September 2023		Italy v Namibia		Stade Geoffroy-Guichard, Saint-Étienne		
14 September 2023		France v Uruguay		Stade Pierre-Mauroy, Lille		
15 September 2023		New Zealand v Namibia		Stadium de Toulouse, Toulouse		
20 September 2023		Italy v Uruguay		Stade de Nice, Nice		
21 September 2023		France v Namibia		Stade de Marseille, Marseille		
27 September 2023		Uruguay v Namibia		Olympique Lyonnais, Lyon		
29 September 2023		New Zealand v Italy		Olympique Lyonnais, Lyon		
5 October 2023		New Zealand v Uruguay		Olympique Lyonnais, Lyon		
6 October 2023		France v Italy		Olympique Lyonnais, Lyon		

2023 Rugby World Cup Fixtures: Pool Games

207

POOL B
South Africa, Ireland, Scotland, Tonga, Romania

MATCH DATE	TEAMS PLAYING		STADIUM		RESULTS
9 September 2023	Ireland v Romania	—	Stade de Bordeaux, Bordeaux	—	
10 September 2023	South Africa v Scotland	—	Stade de Marseille, Marseille	—	
16 September 2023	Ireland v Tonga	—	Stade de la Beaujoire, Nantes	—	
17 September 2023	South Africa v Romania	—	Stade de Bordeaux, Bordeaux	—	
23 September 2023	South Africa v Ireland	—	Stade de France, Saint-Denis	—	
24 September 2023	Scotland v Tonga	—	Stade de Nice, Nice	—	
30 September 2023	Scotland v Romania	—	Stade Pierre-Mauroy, Lille	—	
1 October 2023	South Africa v Tonga	—	Stade de Marseille, Marseille	—	
7 October 2023	Ireland v Scotland	—	Stade de France, Saint-Denis	—	
8 October 2023	Tonga v Romania	—	Stade Pierre-Mauroy, Lille	—	

2023 Rugby World Cup Fixtures: Pool Games

POOL C
Wales, Australia, Fiji, Georgia, Portugal

MATCH DATE	TEAMS PLAYING		STADIUM		RESULTS
9 September 2023	Australia v Georgia	|	Stade de France, Saint-Denis	|	
10 September 2023	Wales v Fiji	|	Stade de Bordeaux, Bordeaux	|	
16 September 2023	Wales v Portugal	|	Stade de Nice, Nice	|	
17 September 2023	Australia v Fiji	|	Stade Geoffroy-Guichard, Saint-Étienne	|	
23 September 2023	Georgia v Portugal	|	Stadium de Toulouse, Toulouse	|	
24 September 2023	Wales v Australia	|	Olympique Lyonnais, Lyon	|	
30 September 2023	Fiji v Georgia	|	Stade de Bordeaux, Bordeaux	|	
1 October 2023	Australia v Portugal	|	Stade Geoffroy-Guichard, Saint-Étienne	|	
7 October 2023	Wales v Georgia	|	Stade de la Beaujoire, Nantes	|	
8 October 2023	Fiji v Portugal	|	Stadium de Toulouse, Toulouse	|	

2023 Rugby World Cup Fixtures: Pool Games

POOL D
England, Japan, Argentina, Samoa, Chile

MATCH DATE	TEAMS PLAYING		STADIUM		RESULTS
9 September 2023	England v Argentina	—	Stade de Marseille, Marseille	—	
10 September 2023	Japan v Chile	—	Stadium de Toulouse, Toulouse	—	
16 September 2023	Samoa v Chile	—	Stade de Bordeaux, Bordeaux	—	
17 September 2023	England v Japan	—	Stade de Nice, Nice	—	
22 September 2023	Argentina v Samoa	—	Stade Geoffroy-Guichard, Saint-Étienne	—	
23 September 2023	England v Chile	—	Stade Pierre-Mauroy, Lille	—	
28 September 2023	Japan v Samoa	—	Stadium de Toulouse, Toulouse	—	
30 September 2023	Argentina v Chile	—	Stade de la Beaujoire, Nantes	—	
7 October 2023	England v Samoa	—	Stade Pierre-Mauroy, Lille	—	
8 October 2023	Japan v Argentina	—	Stade de la Beaujoire, Nantes	—	

2023 Rugby World Cup Fixtures: Pool Games

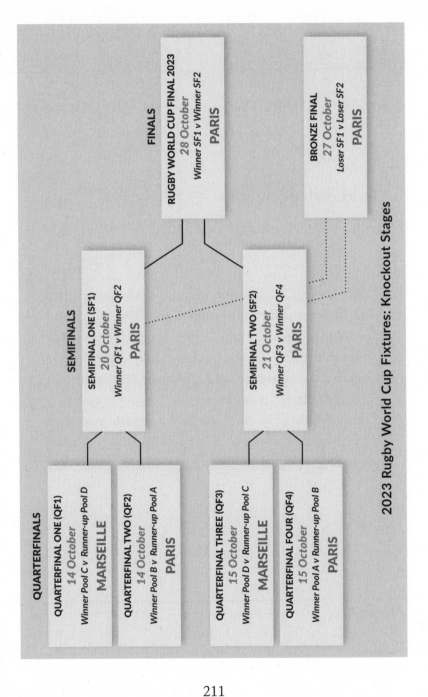

2023 Rugby World Cup Fixtures: Knockout Stages

Acknowledgements

I dedicate this book to my wife, Jane, who has put up with both me and rugby for 45 years. Despite this and her brother, Peter Whipp, being a superb Springbok centre in the late 70s, she has never fully embraced the sport, but acknowledges and appreciates the important part it has played in our lives.

I would also like to thank Lloyd for his help with the structure of the book as well as his hard work and patience in bringing it to fruition.

About the authors

NICK MALLETT is a former Springbok rugby player and was the South African national coach between 1997 and 2000. He was the head coach of Italy's rugby team. He appears regularly on television to comment on rugby, and writes a regular column for Sports24.com.

LLOYD BURNARD is the sports editor of News24. com and the author of *Miracle Men: How Rassie's Springboks Won the World Cup* (Jonathan Ball Publishers, 2020).